THE SEERESS ⊕F PREV⊕RST

"In every generation there appears an individual with the ability to shed a greater light on the path of the seeker. The medium from Prevorst is such an individual. The life and work of Frederika stretches the intellect, rationalizes the ancient teachings, and correlates them with modern spiritual thought. Her knowledge of the ancient 'spiritual inner language' and of concepts both ancient and modern stands the test of time."

REV. SHARON L. SNOWMAN, EXECUTIVE SECRETARY, NATIONAL SPIRITUALIST ASSOCIATION OF CHURCHES

"I believe this book will become a spiritual eye-opener to many, many people. John DeSalvo has brought the Seeress of Prevorst to life."

MARTIN W. STUART PH.D., FORMER PROFESSOR OF MUSICOLOGY, GROSSMONT COLLEGE, SAN DIEGO

The
SEERESS
of
PREVORST

Her Secret Language and
Prophecies from the Spirit World

John DeSalvo, Ph.D.

Destiny Books
Rochester, Vermont

Destiny Books
One Park Street
Rochester, Vermont 05767
www.DestinyBooks.com

Destiny Books is a division of Inner Traditions International

Library of Congress Cataloging-in-Publication Data

DeSalvo, John A.
 The seeress of Prevorst : her secret language and prophecies from the spirit world / John DeSalvo.
  p. cm.
 Includes bibliographical references and index.
 Summary: "Prophecies of a 19th-century German mystic who spent seven years suspended between life and death"—Provided by publisher.
 ISBN 978-1-59477-240-5
 1. Spiritualism. 2. Hauffe, Friederike Wanner, 1801–1829. I. Title.
 BF1283.H3D47 2008
 133.9'1—dc22

2008030755

Printed and bound in the United States by Lake Book Manufacturing

10 9 8 7 6 5 4 3 2 1

Text design and layout by Jon Desautels
This book was typeset in Garamond Premier Pro with Exocet as the display typeface

To send correspondence to the author of this book, mail a first-class letter to the author c/o Inner Traditions • Bear & Company, One Park Street, Rochester, VT 05767, and we will forward the communication.

I dedicate this book to the Seeress of Prevorst,
whose revelations have given new meaning to our
existence and who has explained spiritual
mysteries unknown to us.
I also dedicate it to my wife, Valerie,
and my children, Christopher, Stephen, Paul, and Veronica,
who have supported and encouraged my work.

CONTENTS

PREFACE

S everal years ago, I began to write a book on Abraham Lincoln and his involvement in séances and spiritualism. I thought that this was an important aspect of his life and one that historians had not adequately covered. In my research, I discovered that Abraham Lincoln may have received counsel from one of the best-known spiritualists of that time, Andrew Jackson Davis (1826–1910). Andrew Jackson Davis was considered the founder of modern spiritualism, and most of the beliefs, doctrines, and practices of American spiritualism originated with him. I decided to take some time and learn all that I could about this man. He was the author of more than thirty books, and much source information about him was available to me.

After immersing myself in his work, I was totally amazed to find out that he had predicted many of the astronomical discoveries of the twentieth century. Not only had he predicted the discovery of the planets Neptune and Pluto, but he had come close to predicting the density and number of the moons of Neptune before that planet had even been discovered. He accurately described the surface features of Venus, explained that our solar system also revolves around another center in our galaxy, and detailed the theory of evolution nine years before Darwin ever published *On the Origin of Species*. Davis even suggested the idea of a unified field theory. He also claimed to be able to see the death process and to enter the spiritual realm. I believed that I was the first person to discover these scientific predictions in his writings, so I decided to put aside my book on Lincoln and write one on Davis.[1]

After the publication of that book, I found a statement by him about an individual called the Seeress of Prevorst, born in Germany in 1801, about twenty-five years before Davis's own birth. Like Davis, she claimed to be able to enter higher spheres of consciousness and freely communicate with entities from the spiritual realm. What I found so fascinating about her was that her descriptions of the spirit world were similar to and consistent with Davis's own, and in many cases added a new dimension to them. One of her most incredible claims was that she was able to speak and write in the language of spirits, which she said was the original language of humankind.

In this book, I have included examples of this spirit writing and what we know about it. Could this language reveal mysteries to us and be the "Holy Grail" of communications between our world and the spiritual world? In 1829, the first book about the life and revelations of the Seeress was published, in the German language. The first English translation was published in 1845 and reprinted in English for the last time in 1859. Thus for almost 150 years, this book has been out of print and unavailable to the English-speaking world. The English edition had only one diagram, whereas the original German edition included eight diagrams. The book you have in your hands contains all eight of the original diagrams from the first German edition, as well as illustrations from other sources. In addition, I have obtained all the information I could about the Seeress from nineteenth-century books and magazine and newspaper articles.

It is important to note that many well-known spiritualists and individuals from the nineteenth century acknowledged the true ability of the Seeress to enter higher spiritual realms. These include the Theosophist H. P. Blavatsky, the author Margaret Fuller, the psychic researcher Frank Podmore, and the spiritualists Andrew Jackson Davis and Hudson Tuttle. Certain key individuals involved in secret societies and occult groups seem to have been very interested in her. What drew these powerful occult people to this poor, uneducated peasant woman from an obscure village in Germany? What did she have that was so important to them?

Maybe she knew the mysteries and secrets that they had been searching for all along.

This book tells the story of the Seeress of Prevorst and the spiritual secrets she revealed.

ACKNOWLEDGMENTS

I would like to thank the following libraries and organizations for supplying me with information for my research:

Beinecke Rare Book and Manuscript Library at Yale University
Edgar Cayce Foundation
Hennepin County Library
John Hay Library at Brown University
The National Archives
National Library of Medicine
National Spiritualist Association of Churches
Ouachita Baptist University Library
University of California Libraries
University of Pennsylvania Library

I also would like to extend my sincere thanks to the staff members at the many public and university libraries across the country who assisted me. In addition, I am most grateful to my good friend George Setian in Germany for translating many of the German plates and several sections of the German edition, and for the wonderful photos he took of Prevorst and other areas in Germany, which can be seen in appendix A.

I am particularly indebted to the following individuals for helping me with my research:

Stephen DeSalvo
Dr. J. J. Hurtak
Richard Peterson, Ph.D.
Bob Reissner
Dan Schmidt
Reverend Sharon Snowman

I especially want to thank my very good psychic friends Judy and Marty Stuart, who read the entire manuscript and made invaluable suggestions, and my wonderful editor, Anne Dillon, for the great editing job she did and her dedication throughout the project. No author could ask for a more talented, professional, and kind editor than Anne. I will always be grateful for her labor of love. I would also like to convey my deepest appreciation and gratitude to Jon Graham at Inner Traditions for having faith in this book. Last but not least, I would like to thank my many special friends in Germany, who kindly sent me information, photos, and books about the Seeress.

Quotes about the Seeress of Prevorst

Andrew Jackson Davis (1826–1910), Prophet and Clairvoyant

"I find also many important discoveries and revelations among the Germans—owing very much to their peculiar habits of thinking, and of investigating all seen and unseen laws and operations of Nature; and among them have been persons whose interior perceptions were so unfolded as to enable them to recognize the reality of the spirit world, and its close connection with this rudimental sphere. One should be noticed particularly, because her mind was in a condition occupied by all at the period of death or transformation. She is known as the Seeress of Prevorst and has revealed many truths concerning the connection between the natural and spiritual world and between the soul and the body; and concerning the powers of spiritual perception, and the medium by which the spirit is united with the form. These things are too important to escape the attention of any inquiring mind; for they manifestly involve evidences such as mankind at present need to satisfy them of the powers of the soul, and of other physiological truths."

H. P. Blavatsky (1831–1891),
Founder of Theosophy

"There is also a third possibility of reaching in mystic visions the plane of the higher Manas; but it is only occasional and does not depend on the will of the Seer, but on the extreme weakness and exhaustion of the material body through illness and suffering. The Seeress of Prevorst was an instance of the latter case; and Jacob Böhme, of our second category."

Hudson Tuttle (1836–1910),
Spiritualist and Clairvoyant

"The revelations of different clairvoyants vary; but, in their main features, they coincide as perfectly as can be expected when the ever-changing and extremely subtle conditions of this state are considered. The Seeress of Prevorst was very reliable; and her revelations have a greater significance from the extreme purity and beauty of her spiritual life."

Dr. Justinus Kerner (1786–1862),
Physician to the Seeress

"Regarding the facts which I am about to relate, I have only to say, that, of the great number, I myself was a witness; and that, what I took upon the credit of others, I most curiously investigated and anxiously sought, if by any possibility, a natural explanation of them could be found; but in vain."

Margaret Fuller (1810–1850),
Author of Summer on the Lakes

"Returning to Milwaukee much fatigued, I entertained myself for a day or two with reading. The book I had brought with me was in strong contrast with the life around me. Very strange was this vision of an exalted and sensitive existence, which seemed to invade the next sphere, in contrast with the spontaneous, instinctive life, so healthy and so near the ground I had been surveying. This was the German book entitled:

Die Scherin [*sic*] *von Prevorst* (*The Seeress of Prevorst*). He would be dull who could see no meaning or beauty in the forester's daughter of Prevorst. She lived but nine and twenty years, yet in that time had traversed a larger portion of the field of thought than all her race before in their many and long lives."

Frank Podmore (1856–1910), *Author of* Modern Spiritualism

"The Seeress of Prevorst is responsible for other revelations of a very curious kind. She described, with the utmost minuteness, certain systems of circles—designated respectively Sun Circles and Life Circles—which had relation apparently to spiritual conditions and the passage of time. Kerner gives the most amazing diagrams of these circles and other members of the circle of mystics, which continued for some years to expand and illustrate the revelations of the Seeress, found in this part of her teaching analogies with the philosophical ideas of Pythagoras, of Plato, and of more recent mystics. The characters of this language, as preserved for us in Kerner's plates, bear to the uninstructed eye some resemblance to Hebrew; but they are in many instances quite as complicated as an Egyptian hieroglyph. It was to Hebrew, however, that the Seeress herself, following the example of Dr. Dee's familiars, compared the language; it was, according to her, the primitive universal tongue and resembled the language actually spoken in the time of Jacob."

1

THE LANGUAGE OF THE SPIRITS

During the Renaissance, there was a legend that was especially popular called the Prisca Sapientia, or the Primal Wisdom. It claimed that there was a secret wisdom or knowledge that had been handed down from Adam to Noah to Moses and then through a line of successors, including Pythagoras and Plato. This wisdom was believed to have been the ultimate key for understanding nature, the universe, and the spiritual realm. It was considered the Holy Grail of all knowledge.

This legend was based on the existence of a language called the Primal Language, one that humans could use to communicate directly with the spiritual world and obtain unlimited knowledge. This language was originally revealed to humankind by the angels, and thus it has also been referred to as the Celestial Script.

The holy scriptures of many religions mention angels who reveal some special hidden or mystical knowledge to humankind. One source is the Bible. Although a good part of the Bible is composed of legends, stories, poetry, and allegories, we also find strands of true history encoded in them. I want to make it clear that I don't believe that all of the biblical stories I'm going to relate are actual history; rather, many were mere stories that were used to explain a historical event or an observation. We need to look within the particular story for the historical facts and what they represent.

What does the Bible tell us about the origins of language?

The second chapter of Genesis tells the story of God placing human beings in the Garden of Eden. As we know, the garden had two special trees at its center, the Tree of Life and the Tree of Knowledge of Good and Evil. The former was accessible to humans with God's blessings, the latter was off-limits. We are not informed what kind of knowledge this latter tree would impart to humans, but we can assume it was important, given that the penalty for partaking of the Tree of Knowledge of Good and Evil was death. (I believe that this is the first reference in the Bible to the Primal Wisdom, here called the Tree of Knowledge of Good and Evil.) We also are not told why God did not want humans to possess this knowledge.

We know what happened next: Adam and Eve partook of the fruit of the tree. (In actuality, we do not know what kind of fruit it was. Although we commonly refer to it as an apple, some scholars think it was a fig. This is based on the fact that after Adam and Eve ate the fruit, they sewed fig leaves together to hide their nakedness.) I think this story is trying to tell us that when Adam and Eve were given the Primal Language, they had the opportunity to use it for good or evil.

The specifics of how they were given this knowledge can be found in other ancient sources, which tell us that Adam was given the Primal Language directly from the angels. That is consistent with stories and mythology from other ancient religions. In fact, one ancient tradition even names the angel (Raziel) who gave it to him.

We are then told in Genesis that God asked Adam to name the animals, and whatever name he gave them is what they were then called: "[He] brought them unto Adam to see what he would call them: and whatsoever Adam called every living creature, that was the name thereof."[1] An ancient Jewish tradition teaches that the specific name that Adam gave each animal expressed the animal's true essence. It was more than just a label or title—in a sense, the name *was* the thing. If you knew this name, you had power over it. That is why the Hebrews never pronounced the name Yahweh, which they believed to be the actual or true name of God. To say it or write it down would imply that they had power over him, which would be blasphemy.

Let's assume that Adam was in possession of the Primal Language. From Adam, where did it go? Adam and Eve had at least three sons who are mentioned in the Bible: Cain, Abel, and Seth. Actually, as Genesis 5:4 tells us, they had many more sons and daughters: "And the days of Adam after he had begotten Seth were eight hundred years: and he begat sons and daughters."[2] An apocryphal book called The Second Book of Adam and Eve also discusses the birth of their other children. We know from the Bible that the "spiritual" heir to Adam was his son Seth, born after Cain killed Abel. Thus we can assume that the language went from Adam to Seth. Where did it go next?

Chapter 5 of Genesis contains something that I find very interesting but many Bible scholars find unremarkable. It's a list of descendants, from Adam to Noah, who lived incredibly long lives. For example, Adam lived to the ripe old age of 930, Seth was 912 when he died, Enosh 905, Cainan 910, Mahalalel 895, and Jared was 962. (Jared's son Enoch lived to be only 365, for reasons we will explore.) Most biblical scholars assume that these long life spans did not represent how long these individuals actually lived, but either were an exaggerated age, were symbolic of something else, or even represented the combined ages of individuals in the entire clan or the family.

But perhaps the scholars are wrong. Perhaps these *are* the actual life spans of these individuals, for could it be that the person who possessed the Primal Language also possessed the fountain of youth? Perhaps the timeless search for the fountain of youth has actually been the search for this Primal Language.

Let's pause for a moment to explore the anomaly of Enoch. Why did he die at such a young age of 365 years, compared with the other patriarchs? And *did* he die? It is said that Enoch walked with God. The full text in Genesis says, "And Enoch walked with God: and he was not; for God took him."[3] Thus the legend that surrounded Enoch was that he did not die, but was taken directly up to heaven. Did his possession of this Primal Language prevent him from dying? I believe the Primal Language gave him the ability to enter the spiritual realm at will, and that at one point he decided to leave the Earth and enter heaven. (We will continue our discussion of Enoch a bit later in this book.)

After Enoch, the list of long-lived patriarchs continues: Methuselah lived to be 969 and Lamech lived to 777. Lamech's son was Noah. Almost everyone knows the story of how Noah called the animals into the ark. "There went in two and two unto Noah into the Ark, the male and the female, as God had commanded Noah."[4] If Noah had knowledge of the Primal Language, he would have been able to call the animals by their true intrinsic names and, given the power this granted him, they would have followed him. Indeed, the animals came to Noah as if commanded. Many ancient traditions and tenets of magic are based on names, chants, and mantras; these had real power and could affect physical objects.

Following the story of Noah in the Bible, we have the story of the Tower of Babel. This story of the confusion of languages may be an important clue to what happened to the Primal Language. Perhaps Adam and his immediate descendants up to the time of Noah all shared access to this language, as evinced by this verse from Genesis 11: "And the whole earth was of one language, and of one speech."[5] Humanity was still innocent, and there was no danger in everyone knowing the language. However, as humankind evolved and became more selfish and moved away from the will of God, the language could be used for evil ends by just about anyone, and thus the right to use it eventually became abused.

The story of the Tower of Babel basically tells us that due to this abuse, the language had to be hidden away. This "original language" of humankind appears to have been lost when it was split into other languages. These languages then evolved and changed into the languages that exist today. But was it lost for all time, or could it have been preserved intact and secretly passed down from one person or society to another? It's my belief that it was secretly passed down from one patriarch or society to another to protect it and to keep humanity from abusing it.

Let's continue looking in the Bible for clues to either support or refute this theory. The great prophet Moses may have known this language, and his miracles may have resulted from its use. That he had power over all the animals is made clear in Exodus chapters 7–10, wherein we are told that he was able to command the serpents and cause a plague of locusts, gnats, frogs, flies, and diseases of livestock. It also appears that this language gives one control over nature if one knows the correct intrinsic name for objects. Maybe that's how Moses parted the Red Sea and performed other miracles. If Moses did possess a knowledge of this language, from whom had he received it? Could it have been the Egyptians?

Tradition tells us that Moses was taught the "Secret Doctrines of Egypt." Ancient Egyptians have always been a mysterious culture, one fascinated with death and the afterlife. This interest or obsession may be the result of their familiarity with this ancient knowledge and their ability to communicate with the spiritual world. Perhaps their rites and traditions were based on these esoteric teachings. Some researchers today think that the Great Pyramid may be some kind of device to enter the spirit world or higher dimensions.

The underlying question is: How did this knowledge make its way to Egypt in the first place and eventually to Moses? I believe that from Noah it was eventually passed down through Shem to Abraham. The spiritual heir to Abraham was his son Isaac, and Isaac's spiritual heir was Jacob. The Bible speaks of Jacob talking directly with God and the angels (Jacob's ladder) and God making covenants with him. The Bible clearly states that Jacob entered Egypt and lived there with his family and descendants after his son Joseph was sold to the Egyptians by his brothers (Genesis 37). Thus it is possible that Jacob brought the Primal

Language to Egypt and was responsible for protecting and passing down this tradition and giving it to his son Joseph and to the Egyptians. In this way the knowledge remained in Egypt, guarded by the Egyptian priests, until the time of Moses, when he was taught its use and initiated into it.

There is an interesting alternative route that the Primal Language may have taken. Noah had three sons, Shem, Ham, and Japheth. Our first route that the language may have taken assumed that it was passed to Noah's spiritual heir, Shem, from whom Abraham and the Hebrews descended. But what if something else happened? What if it was passed down, not to Shem, but to one of Noah's other sons instead?

In one of the most amusing stories in Genesis, in chapter 9 we are told that Noah planted the first vineyard and made some wine. He drank too much, and he became drunk. Not only did he become drunk, but he lay naked in his tent. His son Ham, whether by accident or intention, entered the tent and saw his father lying naked and unconscious. He told his two brothers what he had witnessed, and the two brothers entered their father's tent, walking backward so as not to see their father's nakedness, which they then covered with a garment.

Noah then awakens. Discovering what has happened, he is angry at his son Ham for having seen him naked but curses not him, but Ham's son Canaan. That certainly is strange. Why curse the grandson when he is annoyed with the son? It seems unlikely that these people, living close together in a hot climate as they did, taking baths and swimming in the lake together, had never seen one another naked. Given the heat in that region, they probably also slept naked in the summer. Thus it does not seem reasonable that Noah would be outraged because Ham saw him naked.

Why is this silly story even in the Bible?

There must be some hidden message in it. Could it be that all three sons knew that Noah had possession of the Primal Language, and they also knew that only one of them would receive it on Noah's death? Is it possible that when Ham saw that his father was drunk and unconscious, he decided this was his opportunity to sneak into his tent and steal the mystical language? This would be his chance to outdo his brothers and get possession of what his father considered most valuable. That could be why Noah was so angry about what Ham had done. Noah may have previously decided to pass this language to Shem, not Ham or Japheth. Now Ham would possess it also. Or given that Noah could pass it to only one of his sons, now Ham would possess it, which would preclude Noah from giving it to Shem.

Thus, Noah curses Ham's son because Ham and his descendants will have possession of the language when they were not meant to. Is Noah also conveying by this curse that this knowledge will cause Ham's descendants to be evil? Is this what happened? Let's continue with the story.

As we know, Ham's son was Canaan. However, Ham also had three other sons, Cush, Put, and Mizraim. Cush's descendant was Nimrod, who, according to the Bible, was a mighty hunter before the Lord. Was this the case because Nimrod was privy to the Primal Language, which gave him the same control over the animals that Noah had enjoyed? It is also interesting to note that Bible scholars believe that Cush, Mizraim, and Put settled in the Nile River area of Africa. Thus, the descendants of Nimrod had connections to groups in Africa, such as the Egyptians. Perhaps this is another way that the language reached Egypt, and it was there before Jacob came to Egypt. Thus we have two possible routes that the language could have taken when it was passed down from Noah.

It is interesting that if you follow the descendants of Nimrod, you will learn that they were mighty warriors, conquerors, and city builders whose legacy was a rich, cultural one. Was this because they had possession of the Primal Language? Could it be that Nimrod was responsible for the building of the Great Pyramid in Egypt? No one has any idea when and how it was built, owing to the fact that the movement of the bricks and the precision of its construction and inner chambers defy the ability of the ancient Egyptians to have built it in a traditional way. They must have had knowledge of some mystical power or force. Maybe the Primal Language also bestowed the power of levitation, which would have allowed for the large stone blocks to be moved easily into place.

Interesting historical information about the descendants of Ham includes the fact that Nimrod established two kingdoms, one in the land of Shinar and the other in Assyria. These correspond to the kingdoms of the Sumerians, Babylonians, Akkadians, and Assyrians. In fact, Assyria came to be called the Land of Nimrod, and some have suggested that the name Nimrod means "we will revolt." This could imply that he was a mighty leader in rebellion against God. Maybe he used the language for selfish and evil purposes, which was not God's original purpose in giving this language to humankind.

Nimrod established several cities, including Babel, also known as Babylon, meaning "Gate of God." Interestingly enough, this was the site of the Tower of Babel and the confusion of languages. The Tower of Babel was most likely a ziggurat—a tall, pyramid-like structure built in stages, adorned with outside staircases and topped by a religious sanctuary. Given the architectural similarities between the Tower of Babel and the Great Pyramid, perhaps Nimrod *did* build the Great Pyramid in Egypt also, using the power of the Primal Language, as we have suggested above.

If Ham's descendants had access to the Primal Language, were they as extremely long-lived as the earlier patriarchs, who also may have possessed it? What about the other sons of Noah? If we assume that Shem was *not* given the language after Ham had stolen it, what can we find out about the ages of Shem and his descendants? If we assume they did not have the Primal Language, we would guess that their lives would be relatively short (as compared with the much older patriarchs, some of whom lived into the 900s), and in fact, according to the Bible, they were. Shem was 600, his son Arphaxad was 438, and the life spans of their descendants continue to shorten: Salah was 433, Eber was 464, Peleg was 239, Rue was 239, Serug was 230, Nahor was 148, and Terah was 205.

What about Ham and his cursed descendants, who we have speculated may have had access to the Primal Language? Something very interesting happens in the Bible. There are no ages listed in Ham's genealogy. Why not? Perhaps, since this is the accursed line, the writer of this section of the Bible did not want to say anything good about them and so did not disclose their longer lives.

Other ancient legends also make reference to the Primal Language. The Egyptians believed that one of their gods, Thoth, invented writing. He was also considered to be the god of magic and of natural and supernatural knowledge. The Greek god Hermes Trismegistus, sometimes identified as the same Egyptian deity, Thoth, is also described as having this primal knowledge or wisdom. Were they one and the same givers of this Primal Language to humans? The Egyptian priests believed that the words used in magic rituals, this Primal Language, had actual power and produced specific effects, both natural and supernatural. The ritual words could be spoken, chanted, or sung, but in a precise and specific manner. (We will see later that this is a very important aspect of ritual magic.)

One of the most ancient legends of the origin of the Primal Language is from the Kabbalah. This tradition teaches that God gave the angels a secret wisdom known as the Primal Wisdom. After the fall of humankind, this mystical knowledge was then given to Adam by the angels to help him restore his previous standing with God. It was a way to achieve spiritual enlightenment, wisdom, and reconciliation with the creator. Is this not the true goal of all humanity?

It is interesting that the word Kabbalah in Hebrew means "to receive." This knowledge, according to the Kabbalah, eventually disappeared, but generations later God renewed it by giving it directly to Abraham, who eventually passed it down to his son Isaac. Isaac then passed it down to his son Jacob, from whence it went to Joseph, and so on and so forth. The knowledge was then lost again, and, after many generations, God gave it directly to Moses. After Moses, it was again eventually lost. It is important to realize that the Kabbalah tradition states that this knowledge was not written down but instead was orally transmitted from one Hebrew patriarch to another. The Kabbalah tradition is slightly different from my theory in that the Primal Language does not ever get lost but rather is always passed down from one person to the next. Either way, its existence continued.

In the first century CE, Rabbi Shimon Bar Yochai was the first person to have written down one of the books of the Kabbalah. It is called the Sepher Yetzirah and is considered to be the most ancient of all the books of the Kabbalah. It is also known as the Book of Creation. We don't know how he received the information it contains, or if it is the actual teachings of the Primal Wisdom. Other books of the Kabbalah that appeared were the Zohar (The Book of Splendor) and the Bahir (The Book of the Brightness). If these books of the Kabbalah were derived from the original Primal Language, they were most likely edited, diluted, and distorted over the ages. Many study the mystical information in the books of the Kabbalah that we have today, but I do not believe they contain the true mystical meaning and power of their originals, the Prisca Sapientia, or the Primal Wisdom.

Thus we have the existence of several legends, from different cultures and times, about this Primal Language that came to humankind from a deity or from the angels. We have also looked at several possible routes of this language.

But what happened to the language after the time of Moses? We can speculate on many Bible personalities who may have possessed it, but one person for certain is Jesus Christ. Whether you believe Jesus Christ was the son of God or simply a great prophet, the Bible speaks of him performing incredible miracles and commanding both human beings and nature. Only a "word" was needed from him in order to heal. In Matthew, the centurion had such faith in Jesus that he said, "Lord, I am not worthy that thou shouldst come under my roof: but speak the WORD only, and my servant shall be healed."[6] Also, as the Christian Scriptures record, Jesus could transmute elements (change water into wine), had power over life and death (raised Lazarus from the dead), and had control over nature (calmed the storm and walked on water). Whether he knew this inner language because he was God or because it had been passed down to him, it seems that he had knowledge of this Primal Language.

It's interesting to note that there is an apocryphal legend that says that Jesus spent many years in Egypt before his public ministry. It's said that in Egypt he was "being initiated into the Secrets of Egypt." These years—from the time he was twelve until he was thirty, when he began his public ministry—are known as "the lost years of Jesus"; the Bible is silent on them.

From the Dark Ages up until the Renaissance, many mystics, philosophers, and seekers believed this language existed and have searched for it.

We hear about the language again in the twelfth century from the mystic Joachim of Fiore (1130–1202 CE), who predicted what he called the future coming of a "Third Empire of the Holy Spirit." This empire would be the third and final period of human history and the era of the Holy Spirit. In this period, Joachim said the Primal Language of paradise, which names everything by its true essence, would be revealed again, and the mysteries of nature and the spiritual world would be open to all. He did not say precisely when this would occur, but it's known that Christopher Columbus believed in Joachim of Fiore's prophecy. Columbus also believed that the discovery of a new world would hasten the fulfillment of this prophecy. I think most people aren't aware of the fact that one of Columbus's motivations in discovering the New World was related to the Primal Language.

Are these stories pure legend, or could there be some truth to them? Is it possible that this Primal Language really did exist and still does today? Will it reveal, to whoever finds it, all the mysteries of the world and grant unlimited power to its users?

What other references can we find for this Primal Language's existence?

There is an Arabic legend from the Middle Ages that holds that large stones could be levitated by sound and musical vibrations. According to this legend, this was how the Great Pyramid was built. This is another example of a name, or in this case a sound, having power over physical objects. Maybe other megalithic structures like Stonehenge were built this way. Did ancient cultures, like the ones in Central America and other areas of the world, know this Primal Language and use it to build their megalithic structures?

One of my sons, who is a mathematician, said to me, "Instead of the written name or language being the key or intrinsic property to the object or person, it is actually the sound (frequency and resonance) of the thing that is the key. The sound or resonance is what actually causes the change in physical objects or, as legend states, allows you to have power over the object. The written language is just the medium or carrier of the sound, i.e., it is a representation of it."[7]

Moving forward in time, there are other possibilities as to who might have possessed this knowledge, but it is not until the Renaissance that the legend appears again. Who are the candidates at this time? We can only speculate, but a good possibility would be the Knights Templar. If they were in possession of this knowledge, however, they certainly kept it secret. The Church was threatened by their power and persecuted the Knights on political grounds; they were falsely accused of many evil practices. One such practice was of worshipping "a Head." The church made this sound gruesome, implying that the Knights were involved in some kind of perverted worship.

There have been many alternative theories proposed about the true meaning of this symbol of the head. Meanings associated with it include: "being placed at the top, the chief, principal, first, and the top." Could we not define this Primal Language as being first, at the top of all languages, the chief, and the principal one? Maybe the head that the Knights were said to have worshipped was an external symbol of an internal idea or practice, one that, of necessity, had to be disguised in order to be protected. This outward representation of an internal theme is a common practice among secret societies.

It is interesting to note that Sir Isaac Newton knew of this legend of the Primal Wisdom and also believed that his destiny was to be one of the people chosen to receive and understand the Primal Language. Could it also be that Leonardo da Vinci had knowledge of and used this language? I do believe that Leonardo was a recipient of this tradition and that the inspiration for many of his fantastic inventions came from this source. After Leonardo, I believe that the language was continually passed down from one secret society to another, all of which preserved and protected it. From that time to the present, we can only speculate about what may have happened to the Prisca Sapientia. Was this Primal Language completely lost to the world or does it still exist? Where can we next look to find it?

2

INTRODUCTION TO
THE SEERESS

In a small town in Germany in the early 1800s, there lives a young woman, about twenty-five years old, who has been sick for some time. The doctors do not know what is ailing her. Her symptoms are very diverse, and her condition sometimes approaches death. None of their treatments helps, and she continues to get worse.[1]

This young woman is very thin and fragile and has deep, penetrating eyes. Even though she is German, she has an Oriental look and a spiritual radiance that hypnotizes her visitors. Even with her unknown illness, she appears serene and calm and exudes love and warmth. Her family decides to send her to the town of Weinsberg, not too far away, to be treated by a well-known German physician, Dr. Justinus Kerner.

Dr. Kerner was especially well known in Germany for his invention of the ink-blot test, later to be called the Rorschach test after Hermann Rorschach, in the early 1900s, used Kerner's invention to develop the psychological test that would be named for him. Even though today this test is used solely in the field of psychology, Kerner believed that it served as a means to bring him into contact with the spiritual world. Kerner was also an accomplished poet, and it was rumored that he dabbled in mysticism and the occult.

Fig. 2.1. Dr. Justinus Kerner. Image from *Die Seherin von Prevorst und die Botschaft Justinus Kerner,* by Justinus Kerner and von Felix Kretschmar.

Why does Dr. Kerner, a well-known German physician, agree to treat this poor peasant woman? In fact, he eventually invites her into his own home, where he and his wife will treat and take care of her for several years. What was so interesting or unusual about this woman that would cause him to make this commitment to her? Who is this sick young woman? Her name is Frederika Wanner (Hauffe), later to be known as the Seeress of Prevorst.

Even before he met her, Kerner did not believe the reports that he had heard about her. People claimed that she had clairvoyant ability and could speak to ghosts, diagnose illnesses, and even predict events. Most important, she could speak in a strange language that no one could understand.

Fig. 2.2. The Seeress of Prevorst. Image from *Die Seherin von Prevorst und die Botschaft Justinus Kerner,* by Justinus Kerner and von Felix Kretschmar.

After knowing her for a short time, Dr. Kerner was mystified, since much of what she prophesied turned out to be true. Her diagnoses were accurate, her cures for people worked, and most of her predictions were correct. Unusual physical phenomena occurred around her, phenomena sometimes observed by Kerner and others. Initially Kerner tried to ignore and discount these phenomena, but he could not. He was starting to become a believer, but before he went too far, he decided to do what any good doctor would do—he called in experts to get their opinion. But he would not call in just anyone; he would call in those whom he personally knew and trusted. If the Seeress turned out to be a fake or just a hallucinating woman, then no one would know about this except his friends.

In 1863, just one year after Kerner's death, Kerner's biographer, William Howitt, wrote that Kerner was "the most prominent figure in the spiritual circle of Germany."[2] This circle was composed of well-known occultists whom Howitt called "learned metaphysicians and historians," and Kerner was "the chief of these."[3] The experts Kerner called in were part of this circle: Friedrich von Meyer, Gotthilf Heinrich von Schubert, Dr. Carl Ennemoser, Adam Karl August von Eschenmayer, Joseph von Gorres, and Heinrich Werner. They visited Kerner and observed the Seeress.

What were their conclusions? Their verdict was that she was a true seeress who was clairvoyant and could enter the spiritual world. We will discuss these individuals in greater detail a bit later in the book.

What did Kerner and his inner circle want from her? Could she possibly reveal the mysteries of life and death to them? Maybe more important was the fact that she claimed she could write and speak in the language of the spirits. She called it her "inner language" or "the language of the ghosts." She also said it was the same language that Jacob of the Bible spoke. Kerner's eyes must have lit up, since we believe that he was aware of the legend of the Primal Language.

During the two and a half years the Seeress lived in Dr. Kerner's home, he kept notes of the many unusual events that occurred there. He may have been planning to publish this information, and, in fact, within the same year that Frederika died, Kerner did publish the story of her life and revelations, under the title of *Die Seherin von Prevorst: Eröffnungen über das innere Leben des Menschen und über das Hereinragen einer Geisterwelt in die unsere* (The Seeress of Prevorst: Being Revelations

Fig. 2.3. Dr. Justinus Kerner's house. Image from *Die Seherin von Prevorst und die Botschaft Justinus Kerner,* by Justinus Kerner and von Felix Kretschmar.

Concerning the Inner-Life of Man, and the Inter-Diffusion of a World of Spirits in the One We Inhabit).[4] Three German editions were published within the next ten years.

Kerner said that the Seeress believed in her revelations and had vouched for the truth of them on the "seal of death." He also said, "Regarding the facts I am about to relate, I have only further to say, that, of the greatest number, I myself was a witness; and that, what I took upon the credit of others, I most curiously investigated and anxiously sought, if by any possibility, a natural explanation of them could be found; but in vain."[5]

In 1845 the famous Victorian writer Catherine Crowe, author of the book *The Night-Side of Nature: Or, Ghosts and Ghost-Seers* (1848), translated and published the first English version of Kerner's book.[6] She was obviously very interested in the paranormal, having written about it herself. We must be very grateful to her, as this is the first and only English translation ever made. Unfortunately, her translation was not complete—she left out certain sections she thought the public would not be interested in. These sections had to do with the Seeress's inner language and also her sensitivity to metals and other objects. (We have incorporated some of this information into this present book.) Mrs. Crowe's fame helped publicize the book, and it was brought to the attention of the English-speaking world, in both England and America. The last English edition of it was published in 1859. As stated in the preface, for almost 150 years this book has been out of print and not available to the English-speaking world.

Margaret Fuller, a well-known author of the time, is one of those people who read the original German version and were enchanted by it. In her 1843 book, *Summer on the Lakes,* Fuller writes:

> Returning to Milwaukee much fatigued, I entertained myself for a day or two with reading. The book I had brought with me was in strong contrast with the life around me. Very strange was this vision of an exalted and sensitive existence, which seemed to invade the next sphere, in contrast with the spontaneous, instinctive life, so healthy and so near the ground I had been surveying. This was the German book entitled: *Die Scherin* [*sic*] *von Prevorst* (The Seeress of Prevorst).[7]

She then summarizes the book, and it is obvious that she was deeply touched and affected by it. She adds, "He would be dull who could see no meaning or beauty in the forester's daughter of Prevorst. She lived but nine and twenty years [actually the Seeress was twenty-eight when she died], yet in that time had traversed a larger portion of the field of thought than all her race before in their many and long lives."[8]

Many others have also proclaimed the enchanting properties of this book.

3

THE LIFE ⊕F
THE SEERESS

Frederika Hauffe was born on September 23, 1801, in Prevorst, Germany.[1] Prevorst is a forestry hamlet located in the hilly country of Württemberg near Lowenstein. It is about eighteen hundred feet above sea level, in a secluded area. At that time, Prevorst had a population of approximately four hundred inhabitants, whose livelihood depended on woodcutting, coal burning, and collecting the productions of the forest.

Frederika was a lively and happy child, and her parents were the average hardworking people of the time. Her father, Ernest Wanner, was the district forester, and her mother, Frederika Schmidgall, was the daughter of a successful merchant. The family was rather poor, given that her father did not make much money as a forester. Although Frederika seemed normal in most respects, there was definitely something different about her: She was able to see ghosts or spirits. She appeared to have supernatural abilities in her dream state as well as dowsing abilities, not only for finding water but for finding metals and other objects as well: "Thus, on one occasion, when her father had lost some object of value, and threw the blame on her, who was innocent, her feelings being thereby aroused, in the night the place where the things were appeared to her in a dream; and, in her hands, at a very early age, the hazel wand pointed out metals and water."[2]

Her parents were very concerned about her, so when she was five, they sent her to stay with her maternal grandfather, Johann Schmidgall, who lived in Lowenstein, about three miles away. They felt this change might do her some good. During this time, she developed a very close relationship with her grandfather, who was also clairvoyant.

It would appear that many psychics, mediums, and clairvoyants develop a close psychic relationship with one of their grandparents. Edgar Cayce, for example, developed a close relationship with his grandfather, who also had psychic ability. It seems that psychic ability is inherited, and I believe there may be a gene that codes for it. Frederika's second child, who would die at the age of fourteen, also seemed to possess paranormal abilities, as did Frederika's sister. Many times it appears to skip generations, but not always.

Frederika's grandfather immediately recognized Frederika's gifts for clairvoyance. He observed that when she accompanied him on his walks through solitary places, at certain spots a kind of "seriousness and shuddering seemed to seize upon her."[3] He also observed that she experienced the same sensations in churchyards and in churches. This bothered her, and she could not remain in these places for any length of time.*

An event soon occurred that made her grandfather even more aware of her clairvoyant ability.

There was an apartment in the Castle of Lowenstein—an old kitchen—which she [Frederika] could never look into or enter without being much disturbed. . . . To the great regret of her family, this sensibility to spiritual influences, imperceptible to others, soon

---

*It seems that in graveyards, battlefields, and places of violent death, spirits tend to appear. For some reason, the earthly memories found here may cause a spirit to gravitate to these areas. In modern times, scientists using sophisticated equipment have tried to photograph and record the voices of these ghosts. Infrared and ultraviolet photography, digital recordings, and other modern electronic devices have been employed. EVPs, or electronic voice phenomena, are very popular among ghost hunters, who use these digital recorders to capture the voices of the spirits.

became too evident; and the first appearance of a spectre [*spectre* is the term the translator, Catherine Crowe, used for spirit or ghost] to the young girl was in her grandfather's house. There, in a passage, at midnight, she beheld a tall, dark form, which, passing her with a sigh, stood still at the end of the vestibule, turning towards her features that, in her riper years, she well remembered. This first apparition, as was generally the case with those she saw in after life, occasioned her no apprehension. She calmly looked at it, and then, going to her grandfather, told him that 'there was a very strange man in the passage, and that he should go and see him;' but the old man, alarmed at the circumstance—for he also had seen a similar apparition in the same place, though he had never mentioned it—did all he could to persuade her that she was mistaken, and, from that time, never allowed her to leave the room at night.[4]

When Frederika was twelve, she returned home to take care of her parents, both of whom had become ill. She had spent seven years with her grandfather, and we can only guess what transpired during this time. Did he mentor her spirit-seeing abilities and help develop her clairvoyance?

When Frederika was seventeen, the family moved to Oberstenfeld, which is about four miles from Prevorst. A year later she became engaged to Gottlieb Hauffe, a successful merchant, and married him in 1821. (Unfortunately, we know next to nothing about her husband and the details of her personal family life; history has remained silent on this.)

A very significant spiritual experience occurred the day of her marriage. A minister with whom she had developed a very close spiritual relationship was buried that very same day.

It happened that the funeral of the very worthy minister of Oberstenfeld took place on the day of her marriage, a man upwards of sixty years of age, whose preaching, learning, and personal intercourse—

for he was a model of rectitude—had had considerable influence on her life. On the day of the burial, she followed the beloved remains to the churchyard. However heavy her heart was before, at the grave she became light and cheerful. A wonderful inner-life was at once awakened in her; she became quite calm, and could scarcely be induced to quit the grave. At length all tears ceased—she was serene, but, from this moment, indifferent to everything that happened in the world; and, after some indisposition, here began her proper inner-life.[5]

We do not know for sure, but it seems likely that this minister appeared to her in spirit on that day. She hinted about this later in her life. There are many stories of spirits coming back to communicate with their loved ones, so it seems that spirits of the deceased continue to look after us and protect us. The bond of love has no boundaries.

Shortly thereafter, Frederika moved to Kurnbach, about fifteen miles away, to live with her husband at his home. This location did not suit her well, as it was in a gloomy, low-lying area surrounded by mountains. It was just the opposite of Prevorst and Oberstenfeld, where she had lived most of her life. Within a year of this move, she developed an unknown illness. We don't know for certain what caused this, but the elevation of her new location may have been a factor. Typically, she reacted negatively to lower geographical areas like Kurnbach and was positively affected by high geographical areas like mountain regions.

It's interesting to note that as Frederika's illness progressed, her clairvoyant abilities increased, as did the frequency with which she was able to enter into the spiritual realm. Sometimes she seemed to approach death. The physicians who tried to help her just made her worse, since they didn't know what was ailing her, and their medical treatments were very primitive. At this time, Frederika's clairvoyant abilities consisted of being able to see people and objects in crystals and mirrors; predict the immediate future, including the imminent deaths of family members and friends; have prophetic dreams and second sight; and see and communicate with spirits. Most of her family and friends believed that she was hallucinating. As time passed, the spirits appeared to her more frequently.

She tried as best she could to carry out her duties as wife to a successful merchant, but whenever possible she would flee to solitude to retire into herself. She tried to hide her spiritual experiences from family and friends but found it increasingly difficult to do so. It's possible that this battle between her physical and spiritual existence wore on her, and this continual inner conflict, coupled with the detrimental effects of the physical environment of her new home, worked together to produce her illness. This illness and her clairvoyant ability were with her for the next seven years, until she died.

As stated, the Seeress often experienced clairvoyant and prophetic dreams. On the night of February 13, 1822, she had a strange dream about being in her room with a dead man. This man was someone who was dear to her, who had kindled her inner life when he was alive (most likely it was the minister). In this dream, in a room next to hers, her father and two physicians were discussing her condition and how to cure her. She cried out that no physician could cure her, but "only this dead man." Many nights during her illness her grandmother appeared to her, standing by her bedside and looking silently at her. The Seeress recognized her as her protecting spirit. Thus it appears these dreams indicated that her help would come from the spiritual world and not from any physician.

At about this time, she dreamed of a strange machine that she said would cure her. After describing it in detail, she drew a diagram of it on paper, but no one paid any attention to it. She explained that the vision of this machine was given to her in her dreams by her protecting spirit.

Years later and shortly before her death, Kerner constructed this machine. It appears to have been some kind of electric or galvanic apparatus. Dr. Kerner, on studying it, thought that if she had used it at the time of her illness, she would most likely have been cured. The Seeress

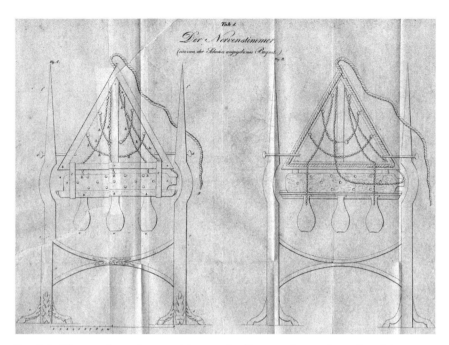

Fig. 3.1. The machine that would cure the Seeress. Image from *Die Seherin von Prevorst: Eröffnungen über das innere Leben des Menschen und über das Hereinragen einer Geisterwelt in die unsere.*

said this machine would have "charged her nerves," and she called it *der Nervenstimmer,* or the nerve-tuner. A photograph of this nerve-tuner can be found in appendix A.

Since most of the traditional medical remedies proved useless to heal the Seeress, some less traditional methods were tried. Some physicians and other practitioners used mesmerism to cure patients in the nineteenth century. This practice utilized magnetic passes to equalize a person's energy field (and will be discussed in greater detail in the following chapter). This seemed to help her for a period of time. Homeopathy was also tried. This is a system that treats "like with like." Its premise is that chemicals that produce symptoms of illness in healthy individuals can cure patients ill with that condition when they are given very low doses of the same chemical substance. Homeopathic physicians believe that the potency of a remedy can be increased by diluting the dosage to a point where it is possible that not even a molecule of the original ingredient is present.

In February 1823, Frederika gave birth to her first child, a boy. It's remarkable that during the first week of his life, he always slept in the same position that she assumed during her magnetic sleep or clairvoyant state, namely, with his arms and feet crossed. Unfortunately, the child died six months later, in August. Her illness got worse after his death, and at this point she was extremely debilitated, had lost her teeth, and was suffering from hemorrhages. The medicines and remedies prescribed by various doctors did not help her and, in fact, seemed to make her worse. Her friends tried everything to make her better and even called in a person who used something they called "Sympathy" or "Sympathetic Magic" to cure people. He gave her an amulet, but his treatment only aggravated her illness.

Dr. Kerner describes her condition at the time:

Whereupon, she was so much affected, that she became as cold and stiff as a corpse. For a long time no respiration was perceptible; at length there was a rattling in her throat. Baths and other remedies were applied, and she revived, but only to continued suffering. She always lay as in a dream. At one time, she spoke for three days only in verse; and at another, she saw for the same period nothing but a ball of fire that ran through her whole body as if on thin bright threads. Then for three days she felt as if water was falling on her head, drop by drop; and it was at this time that she first saw her own image. She saw it clad in white, seated on a stool, whilst she was lying in bed. She contemplated the vision for some time, and would have cried out, but could not. At length she made herself heard, and on the entrance of her husband it disappeared.[6]

Her clairvoyant ability also seemed to increase during this illness: "Her susceptibility was now so great, that she heard and felt what happened at a distance; and was so sensible [sensitive] to magnetic influences, that the nails in the walls annoyed her, and they were obliged to remove them. Neither could she endure any light."[7]

This hearing and seeing at a distance appears to be what we call "remote viewing" today. This is being able to project your consciousness or spirit to a remote location. Thus you can physically be in one place but have your consciousness in a distant location. The famous Catholic priest and stigmatic Padre Pio seemed to have had this ability.

Frederika was placed under the care of a physician referred to as Dr. B. This physician prescribed magnetic passes and also medicines, but she continued to fall into the clairvoyant state and prescribe for herself. This is very similar to what happened to Edgar Cayce. When he was young, he developed an unknown throat ailment and could barely speak. In one of his first trance states, Cayce diagnosed and prescribed for himself. This remedy immediately cured his throat problem and he was able to speak. Later, he diagnosed and prescribed for others this way, as did other clairvoyants in the nineteenth century, including Andrew Jackson Davis.

It also appears that Frederika received spiritual help at this time.

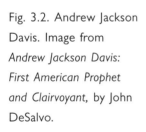

Fig. 3.2. Andrew Jackson Davis. Image from *Andrew Jackson Davis: First American Prophet and Clairvoyant*, by John DeSalvo.

For seven days, at seven o'clock in the evening, she felt she was being magnetized by a spirit who was visible only to her. She recognized this spirit as her grandmother, who magnetized her with three fingers outspread like rays, the passes being directed toward her stomach area. In her clairvoyant state, Frederika declared that only mesmerism, or magnetism, as she called it, could save her.

Strange physical phenomena were also observed near her during this time: "It is an incomprehensible circumstance, though believed by many trustworthy persons, that during this period, articles whose near neighborhood to her was injurious, were removed by an unseen hand; such objects—a silver spoon, for example—would be perceptibly conveyed from her hand to a more convenient distance, and laid on a plate; not thrown, for the things passed slowly through the air, as lifted by invisible agency."[8]

This is what is called a poltergeist phenomenon; it is thought to be caused by a spirit that makes its presence known by moving or throwing objects that make noise. The term comes from the German terms for "to knock" and "spirit" and is sometimes referred to as "a noisy ghost." It was about this same time that Frederika, when looking at a person, would see another person directly behind the one she was looking at. No one else would see this other person. Behind her youngest sister, she saw their deceased brother, Henry. Behind a lady friend she saw the ghostly form of an old woman, who had been a friend of this lady in childhood. (Again we have a description of deceased relatives or close friends from the spirit world protecting and guiding a loved one.)

Frederika's spiritual experiences intensified. She could predict events by looking into a glass of water or mirror. Today this ability is called scrying, and it includes staring into crystals (crystal gazing), regular or black mirrors, and clear or dark fluids. Dr. Kerner gives an example of her scrying ability:

> Thus, in a glass of water that stood upon the table, she saw some persons, who, half an hour afterwards, entered the room. She also saw,

in the same manner, a carriage traveling on the road to B., which was not visible from where she was. She described the vehicle, the persons that were in it, the horses, etc; and in half an hour afterwards this equipage arrived at the house. At this time she seemed also endued [endowed] with the second sight. One morning, on leaving the room during the visit of her physician, she saw a coffin standing in the hall, which impeded her way; in it lay the body of her paternal grandfather. She returned, and bade her parents and physician come out and see it; but they could see nothing, nor, at that time, she either. On the following morning the coffin, with the body in it, was standing by her bedside. Six weeks afterwards the grandfather died, having been in perfect health until a few days of his death.[9]

Frederika's condition continued to grow worse, and she could hardly sit up. When encouraged to get out of bed, she would fall flat to the ground. Her family and friends became frustrated, since nothing seemed to help. Finally they began to believe that her illness was been caused by demonical influences. Throughout history, strange and inexplicable phenomena have been blamed on the devil; apparently the same thing happened here.

Her family decided to call in another man who practiced magic. This man gave her a green powder, which she initially refused before ultimately being forced to take it. When she was administered the powder a second time, she improved a little and was able to stand. But a short while later, she started to run uncontrollably in a circle. This event was the catalyst for what I believe is the most significant phenomenon in the life of the Seeress: She started speaking in a strange language, which she called her inner language or language of the spirits.

Kerner describes this language that she spoke: "She was now never thoroughly awake; her voice was shrill; she spoke High German (she had never learned this), and a strange language, which she also wrote, and which she called her inner tongue, of which we shall speak further. When she spoke this language she was in a half-waking state; and when she wished to speak in the ordinary manner, she made some magnetic passes on herself."[10]

The magnetic passes mentioned are those used in the process of mesmerism, whereby the mesmerist moves his hands up and down and sometimes sideways along a subject to effect their magnetic field and put the subject in a magnetic state or trance. The green powder she was given seemed to help induce this state, which she claimed made her "more magnetic." She also believed that the intentions of the man who gave her the green powder may not have been the best. Perhaps he wanted to use her spiritual abilities for selfish ends. For some reason, Frederika didn't want this man to get physically close to her, and she said that she took the powder in small doses "lest the man should bring mischief on [me]." He also gave her a strange-looking amulet to help her. Strange things happened in conjunction with this amulet, which would "occasionally, of its own accord, untouched by any one, run about her head, breast, and bed-covering, like a living thing, so that they had to pick it up from the floor and restore it to her. This incredible circumstance happened in the presence of many trustworthy witnesses, who testify to the fact. She wore this amulet on her back for a quarter of a year."[11]

Later, when she was committed to Dr. Kerner's care, he examined the amulet and found that it contained asafetida, sabina, cyanus, two stramonium seeds, a small magnet, and a piece of paper, on which were written the words: "The Son of God came to destroy the works of the devil!" Did this amulet actually move of its own accord? From the witnesses, Dr. Kerner believed that it did.

Frederika continued to be attacked by an extreme irritability of the stomach and had to eat something almost every minute or she would fall into an alarming state of weakness. Medicines did not help. Her family decided to bring her to her uncle at Lowenstein. Every evening she would go into her clairvoyant state and prescribe for herself, but no one placed any confidence in her prescriptions, and they were not followed. Her friends believed she was possessed by demons, and they tried to exorcise them by prayer. Nothing seemed to work, and she became more withdrawn and indifferent to her physical surroundings.

It was at this point that Frederika's family moved her to Weinsberg to be under the care of the illustrious Dr. Kerner. Frederika arrived at Weinsberg on November 25, 1826. When she arrived, Kerner observed that she was a picture of death, wasted like a skeleton, and unable to rise or lie down without assistance. About every three or four minutes it was necessary to give her a spoonful of broth to keep her from fainting. A description of her condition by Dr. Kerner follows. Note that he does not want to admit to her clairvoyance and insists that she be treated with traditional medical means.

> It was at this time I was called in to her. I had never seen her, but I had heard many false and perverted accounts of her; and I must confess that I shared the world's opinions, and gave credit to its lies. I therefore desired that no notice whatever should be taken of her magnetic state, nor of her directions to treat her magnetically, and place her in relation with people of strong nervous temperament—in short, I desired that everything should be done to draw her out of the magnetic condition—that she should be treated carefully, but by ordinary medical means.[12]

Unfortunately for Kerner, however, every conventional remedy he tried produced an undesirable effect and she got worse: "But the very smallest doses of medicine always produced in her effects the reverse of what I expected; she was attacked by many alarming symptoms, and it appeared probable that her end was approaching; and for this result her friends were fully prepared. In short, it was too late for the plan I proposed to be of any service to her."[13]

Since Kerner's treatment didn't seem to help, he gave up after a few weeks. Feeling that he had nothing to lose, he allowed her to prescribe her own treatment, which would come to her during her clairvoyant state. (She could prescribe only in this state and not in her normal conscious state.) Usually she would enter the clairvoyant state every morning at seven, beginning with silent prayer. She would then close her eyes and cross her arms over her chest. After a while, she would spread her arms straight outward, and it was at this point that she fully entered into the clairvoyant state. She would then place her arms back on the bed and begin to speak.

During a trance, her face would appear calm, serene, and transfigured. Kerner was amazed and also embarrassed that her remedies were much better for her than his traditional medical treatments had been. During the time she was under his care until her death, she continued to prescribe for herself, and, fortunately for us, Kerner watched and recorded these extraordinary events.

The Seeress eventually moved into Kerner's home, on April 6, 1827, and lived there permanently as a patient except for a short time before her death. Both Dr. Kerner and his wife took care of her and attended to her needs. Her fame spread all over the country, and many people visited her for cures, but also out of curiosity. Even though this was a burden to her, she helped anyone in any way she could.

Frederika requested that magnetic passes or mesmerism be used as a treatment for her. Since Kerner still did not want to be part of this type of treatment, he employed a friend of his to make the magnetic passes on her every day for seven days. The result of this was that Frederika was able to sit up in bed, feeling stronger than she ever had under medical treatment. This magnetic treatment continued for twenty-seven more days, and while Kerner realized that she would probably never be restored to perfect health, many of her distressing symptoms were much relieved. Unfortunately, as she was getting better, she received the bad news that her father had died. This shocked her terribly and counteracted the beneficial influence of the magnetic treatments.

Dr. Kerner started to realize that something incredible was going on. He stated that in her clairvoyant state, "she was then much more really awake than other people; for this condition, although it is not called so, is that of the most perfect vigilance."[14] He finally admitted she was in some high spiritual state of being. This is an important statement for him to make, because it indicates a shift in his attitude toward her and her gifts. Although when in a trance Frederika appeared to be in a state of stupor, she was more awake than the average person: she was in a state with a higher awareness and had a higher level of consciousness.

Thus we see a remarkable transformation occurring in Dr. Kerner during the two and a half years that he was with the Seeress. The world is very fortunate that he was the physician called in, since a different doctor might not have had the humility and openness to admit and recognize the amazing powers of this woman. How many people like her have been lost to the world because they were not acknowledged or recognized by others?

4

MESMERISM AND HYPNOSIS

F rederika had been mesmerized many times in her life and believed
that only mesmerism could help her. In Germany at that time this
treatment was not unusual. Let's look at this process and its history.

The person who is considered to be the discoverer of the technique
of mesmerism is Franz Anton Mesmer, an Austrian physician (1733–
1815). He believed that all animals and humans could be influenced
or affected by an invisible magnetic force. This force was called animal
magnetism, which is from the French *magnétisme animal*. If used prop-
erly, it could be a healing agency. Mesmer believed that the magnetic
force was carried by a magnetic fluid. He developed and popularized
this theory in the late eighteenth century and first published it an article in 1779 entitled *Mémoire sur la découverte du magnétisme animal*
(Propositions Concerning Animal Magnetism).

The mesmeric technique for healing was as follows: Patients sat
around a large tub full of magnetized water in which various substances,
including herbs and other chemicals, had been dissolved. Rods or ropes
extended from the vat and each patient held the end of one of these.
Sometimes the rope was wrapped around the affected part of the body.
The magnetic force produced from the vat traveled through the rod or
rope and entered a person to effect a cure.

There were many variations on this process. Sometimes the people who participated in it experienced trancelike states, convulsions, laughter, crying, and other violent emotions. Some became insensitive to pain, or carried out suggestions by the magnetizer. Some even exhibited unusual psychic ability. Some claimed to be cured, but not all were. Mesmer believed the process worked because this force redistributed the magnetic fluid flowing through a person's body to its natural and harmonic state, thus healing the person of his ailments. The technique traveled to England and other parts of Europe, and in the mid-1800s it came to the United States. It eventually became known as mesmerism, named after its founder.

A very interesting development occurred in 1784. Armand de Puységur, a student of Mesmer, found that from this mesmeric state one could enter into a deeper trance that produced a higher state of awareness. This deeper trance state would later be called clairvoyance. While in this state, a person might appear to be sedated or asleep, but would actually be very lucid.

Clairvoyance is defined as the power or ability to discern objects not present to the senses and/or the ability to perceive matters beyond the range of ordinary perception. It is an intuitive insight into the nature of things. It is sometimes referred to as "clear seeing," "second sight," or even "extrasensory perception (ESP)." Clairvoyance is a catchall term for anomalies such as precognition, visions, telepathy, mediumship ability, remote viewing, prophecy, psychometry, and other paranormal abilities. It was often the case that people in the clairvoyant state had diagnostic and self-healing capabilities, both for themselves and for others of whom they had no knowledge. Sometimes it was possible for a person to enter this state spontaneously, without any apparent cause, but only for brief periods of time.

Another way to access the clairvoyant state was by employing the special technique of hand passes. This initially allowed for the person to be mesmerized before the trance was deepened and the subject moved into the clairvoyant state.

In 1842 James Braid coined the term *hypnotism,* meaning, in Greek, "putting to sleep," to describe the process of mesmerism. I believe this was a real injustice, because, as we shall see, there is a real difference between mesmerism and hypnotism. Throwing mesmerism into the category of hypnosis—which is a completely different state of consciousness—was the beginning of the suppression of the true capabilities of mesmerism and clairvoyance. My guess is that at first, hypnosis *did* use the techniques of mesmerism and its hand passes, but as time went on, the use of the passes was dropped and other techniques like gazing and visualization were used instead.

The primary difference between mesmerism and hypnotism is that while mesmerism can lead to the clairvoyant state, hypnosis typically cannot. Modern hypnosis, as stated, does not employ the technique of hand passes, a technique that must be utilized to enter the state of mesmerism and, following that, the state of clairvoyance. The passes are necessary to redistribute the magnetic fluid, which is not a factor in the hypnotic process.

In the first stages of mesmerism, the behavior of the person being mesmerized *may* be similar to that of hypnosis. He or she may be insensitive to pain or may do things at the request of the operator. But this is not a hypnotic stage; it is an early mesmeric stage caused by the operator acting on the person's mesmeric fluid. As this mesmeric stage deepens, it may lead to clairvoyance. The deepening of the hypnotic state will most likely *not* lead to clairvoyance.

I hope this clarifies the difference. It all boils down to the magnetic fluid in the body and manipulating and redistributing that. Hypnosis does not engage the physical fluid but rather is a mental process that works on a person's conscious and subconscious levels. I would like to quote an important section from John Barter regarding this distinction:

> Clairvoyance is the perception of things distant either in time or in space. It may be divided into two parts, *previsional,* and *spacial.* Through previsional clairvoyance, forthcoming events are foretold.

By spacial clairvoyance things are seen when placed in such a position that normally they are invisible. Thus, a clairvoyant sitting in one room may tell the name of every article, even the smallest, in another room, although he could not possibly have known or seen them previously. It has since been proved that clairvoyance cannot proceed from the hypnotic state at all, it can only be deduced from mesmerism. It can only be developed in a sensitive by repeated mesmeric processes, which may require several weeks. Very few sensitives become clairvoyant; to arrive at this stage requires careful cultivation and tact on the part of the mesmerist.[1]

Today, hypnotism is used by medical doctors and psychologists to induce a trance state to relax the mind and body and open up a person's subconscious mind. The truth is that while few psychologists agree on what hypnosis really is, most concur that it produces some type of altered state of consciousness. Most medical practitioners are also not aware of additional higher states of consciousness that may exist beyond the hypnotic state.

It is unfortunate that after the nineteenth century most doctors rejected clairvoyance and accepted only the existence of hypnotism. They never went beyond this. What a different world it would be today if the doctors and scientists at that time had accepted the existence of the clairvoyant state and used it for all types of applications—from diagnosis, to treatment, to prophecy.

As mentioned, some well-known individuals who claimed to be able to enter the clairvoyant state were the prophet Edgar Cayce[2] and Andrew Jackson Davis,[3] the founder of modern spiritualism. When in this state, these individuals were able to diagnose and prescribe for themselves as well as for strangers. They were uncannily accurate in their diagnoses and the forms of treatment they suggested. Modern medical doctors who have studied them are astonished that many of their treatments were years ahead of their time.

The most amazing story I ever heard about Edgar Cayce concerned a reading in which he prescribed a remedy for a person with a leg sore. In a trance, Edgar said to use "oil of smoke" to cure the leg. No one knew what this product was and it couldn't be found anywhere. The next time Edgar was in a trance, he was asked where this "oil of smoke" might be procured. He named a specific drugstore in Louisville, Kentucky. Upon inquiry, however, the manager of the store said he had never heard of anything by that name. When in trance again, Cayce said that the drug was in the back room of that drugstore, and even described its exact location on a specific shelf. The manager looked on that specific shelf and found an old bottle whose label was faded. He picked it up and read the label. It said "Oil of Smoke."[4] He had no idea he even had it. There is no way to explain this by normal means, and I believe it is a good example of true clairvoyant ability.

In the nineteenth century, it was commonly believed that if one was mesmerized many times, one would eventually enter the clairvoyant state. It seems the more you try it, the more likely you are to succeed. Thus many of the books and manuals published about mesmerism gave specific instructions for mesmerism and clairvoyance.

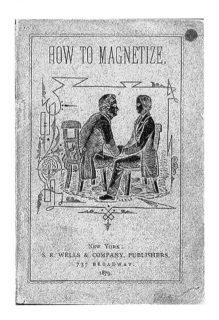

Fig. 4.1. An 1879 pamphlet on magnetism. Image from *How to Magnetize,* by James Victor Wilson.

An interesting modern application of this theory of a magnetic fluid or field affecting the human body is the use of magnetic bracelets, mattresses, and therapies. Most physicians doubt the efficacy of these treatments, but many people swear by the results they get. I personally have used a magnetic bracelet and was surprised at the beneficial results it produced. Initially I didn't believe it would have any effect, but it did.

Mesmerism has fascinated me for years, and I have collected as many nineteenth-century books as possible on the topic. I'd like to describe the stages of mesmerism as explained in these books, while prefacing this by saying the procedure of mesmerism shouldn't be attempted by anyone unless he or she is a licensed physician trained in hypnosis. This is just a brief summary for informational and historical purposes.

Before defining the stages, we need to define a few terms used in the process. The person who mesmerizes is called the *operator,* and the person being operated on or mesmerized is called the *subject.* When the subject enters the mesmeric state, he is then called the *sensitive.*

Mesmerism involves six main stages, and they usually follow in order, but not necessarily.[5] The procedure of passing hands over the person to induce the mesmeric state may take as long as an hour, but may require much less time if the person is a receptive subject.[6]

1. *The waking stage* (illustration no. 1, figure 4.2). The operator has not yet produced any apparent change in the subject. No unusual phenomena are observed, although the subject may have been affected.

2. *The transition stage* (illustration no. 2, figure 4.2). The sensitive (we now call the subject the sensitive since he or she has entered the early mesmeric state) is under imperfect or incomplete control of the operator. Vision is the only one of the senses that is impaired in the transition stage. The mental faculties still remain under the control of the sensitive.

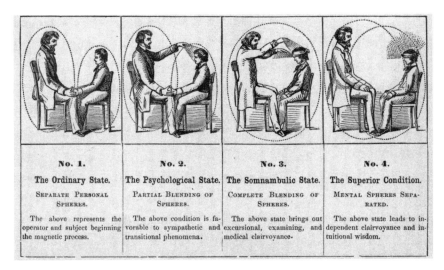

No. 1.	No. 2.	No. 3.	No. 4.
The Ordinary State.	**The Psychological State.**	**The Somnambulic State.**	**The Superior Condition.**
SEPARATE PERSONAL SPHERES.	PARTIAL BLENDING OF SPHERES.	COMPLETE BLENDING OF SPHERES.	MENTAL SPHERES SEPARATED.
The above represents the operator and subject beginning the magnetic process.	The above condition is favorable to sympathetic and transitional phenomena.	The above state brings out excursional, examining, and medical clairvoyance.	The above state leads to independent clairvoyance and intuitional wisdom.

Fig. 4.2. The primary stages of mesmerism. Image from *The Great Harmonia,* by Andrew Jackson Davis.

3. *The sleeping stage.* The mesmeric sleep is complete, and the sensitive's mind can now be influenced by the operator. The sensitive is also unconscious to pain.

4. *The somnambulistic or sleep-waking stage* (illustration no. 3, figure 4.2). The sensitive is awake but still deep in the trance and can think or act only as permitted by the operator. In a sense, the subject wakes up within himself or herself, thinking, seeing, and hearing as permitted by the operator. This is the stage in which experiments on the sensitive can begin.

5. *The clear sleep-waking or lucid somnambulistic stage* (illustration no. 4, figure 4.2). This is the most unusual stage and the most difficult to achieve. The sensitive now manifests clairvoyance, that is, thought-reading or reading someone's mind, and can also make an internal inspection of another person for medical purposes. The sensitive has knowledge of his or her bodily and mental state and can diagnose and prescribe for himself or herself and for others.

6. *The spiritual stage* (illustration no. 4, figure 4.2). The sensitive

passes completely beyond the control of the operator. This stage is extremely rare. The person in this stage has knowledge of the laws of the universe and spiritual revelations. It is the stage of the prophet, seer, and seeress who reveal new mysteries to humankind. This is the stage that was reached by the Seeress of Prevorst and by Andrew Jackson Davis.

The invisible substance being manipulated is also called the mesmeric aura. Every human being possesses it to a greater or lesser degree. The mesmeric sleep is produced by this invisible substance, which proceeds from the operator and electrifies or wakes up the sensitive. In theory, all individuals can mesmerize someone, and all individuals can be mesmerized by someone.

It's very interesting that an old pamphlet on mesmerism lists the criteria for the best subjects to mesmerize.[7] They include young females who are weak and possibly debilitated. This certainly describes the Seeress's condition. Since mesmerism played such a role in the Seeress's life, and this process led to her clairvoyance, it's important to look at the details of the technique and how it was applied.

It has been stated that the mesmeric sleep is produced by the mesmeric aura. There were several ways that a mesmerist would apply the technique, including the method of making both downward and upward passes, which was the most widely used. The downward pass had the effect of inducing sleep and putting the subject into the mesmeric state. The upward pass produced the reverse effect in that it was capable of awakening the subject from the mesmeric sleep.

To start, the subject should be sitting in a comfortable armchair. The operator should stand or sit opposite in a slightly higher chair and should try to make the subject feel relaxed and at home and not have any fear or anxiety. The operator's knees should touch the subject's. The operator then takes the subject's thumbs between thumb and finger so that the interior of the operator's thumb touches the interior of the subject's thumb. Then the operator should look steadily into the subject's eyes, blinking as little as possible. (Some mesmerists preferred that subjects close their eyes or be blindfolded at a certain stage in the process and others preferred that the eyes stay open.) The operator remains in this position for two to five minutes. The operator then withdraws the hand, extends the fingers over the subject's head, and begins the series of passes.

The operator then stretches out both hands at full length with the fingers extended and pointed to the eyes of the person at a distance of about three inches, the backs of the hands being naturally upward. The operator then slowly brings both hands down to the feet; this is the downward magnetic pass. The operator then opens the hands before bringing them back, not the same way, but with a circular motion on each side of the chair, until they are raised to the original position. The operator should use mind energy or intention to put the subject to sleep. The upward passes are never done in front of the body, because then there would be an upward pass that would undo the work of the downward pass.

After doing this for a while, the operator should feel the tips of the fingers tingle with the sensation of the mesmeric aura escaping from them. These passes should be done slowly, at the rate of about ten passes per minute. If done too rapidly, they will produce a current of air that for some reason has the effect of delaying the mesmeric sleep. The passes are made as close as possible to the subject's face and body without touching the subject. This process should continue for about twenty minutes, or until the subject falls into a mesmeric sleep. If unsuccessful after twenty minutes, the session should be terminated and tried again later.

As soon as the subject falls into the mesmeric trance, the operator can begin asking questions. When this phase is over, the session is ended by the operator applying upward passes to the sensitive. Usually just a few of these are enough to awaken the subject.

Let me give more details of the passes, as these are the main elements in this process. The following is a description by John Barter:

The downward pass has the effect of inducing sleep; all downward passes extend from the head to a little below the breast, but occasionally a more prolonged one should be made, from head to feet, for the purpose of equalizing the mesmeric aura; there are also downward local passes, made from the head to the shoulders, the sides of the head, etc; but all downward passes induce the mesmeric sleep.

The upward pass is made the reverse way to the above; commence a little below the breast, the backs of the hands towards the ground, palms upward, fingers extended; raise both hands as high as the head; open both hands and bring them up by the sides of the patient with a circular motion; continue this practice. Upward passes have the effect of awakening the subject from the mesmeric sleep.[8]

We know that the Seeress was mesmerized many times in her life. Was this a contributing factor to her developing clairvoyance and her ability to reach the spiritual stage? I'm sure it played a part. Also, her health and other factors must have contributed. The quotation from H. P. Blavatsky at the beginning of this book bears repeating here: "There is also a third possibility of reaching in mystic visions the plane of the higher Manas; but it is only occasional and does not depend on the will of the Seer, but on the extreme weakness and exhaustion of the material body through illness and suffering. The Seeress of Prevorst was an instance of the latter case; and Jacob Böhme of our second category."[9]

So did all these factors contribute to the Seeress's ability to enter the clairvoyant state, or is there something beyond this that we are not aware of? It's my hypothesis that at first the Seeress employed a human operator to enter into this mesmeric state and possibly the higher spiritual stage. Then she claimed that spirits mesmerized her. Finally, she did not need an operator or spirits to enter the mesmeric state and could enter the higher spiritual stage at will. Few people in our history had this gift and ability.

5

CLAIRV⊕YANCE

There have been many terms used to describe the paranormal abilities of the Seeress, but I believe the most accurate one is *clairvoyance*. It is also very interesting that in Catherine Crowe's 1845 English translation of Kerner's book, she writes in the preface that this book would have a deep interest for those who believe in clairvoyance.

Dr. Kerner and others at that time used several different terms for the clairvoyant state.[1] Sometimes he used the term *somnambulism,* but not in the medical sense of sleepwalking, that is, while the person is asleep or in a sleeplike state, he or she engages in activities that are normally associated with wakefulness. Rather, he used the terms *somnambulism, sleep-waking* (not *sleep-walking*), *magnetic sleep,* and *mesmerism* interchangably to refer to the higher consciousness and expanded awareness of the spiritual world into which the Seeress was capable of entering. When you come upon these terms in quotes by Dr. Kerner and others, I suggest you replace them with *clairvoyance*.

Dr. Kerner described this enlightened state as being the most perfect awake state. It is the rising of a bright, inner sun, in which your awareness is clearer than in your waking state. He explains it as follows:

> I will, in this place, say a few words on the existence of that inner life which is called the magnetic sleep—a subject which the con-

tents of this book will more fully explain. We must not call this condition sleep—it is rather a state of the most perfect vigilance; for it is the rising of an inward and much brighter sun than that which our external eyes behold, and it is lighted by a clearer light than our waking life can furnish by means of our ideas, conclusions, definitions, and systems. It is a condition which resembles the primitive state of mankind, when man lived in intimate connection with nature, understood her laws, and read her in her original type.[2]

As he notes, clairvoyance is not a new state but a state that early humans had the ability to enter into in a natural manner. It was an innate ability at that time.

Some mystics believed that before the fall of humankind, the soul had an intuitive knowledge and a prophetic gift of immense power. Today the soul still possesses these abilities and powers, but they are not perceptible. In sleep, however, when our inward inspiration is not repressed, this magic power is aroused. In sleep, we let go of our ego, and that inner light is more accessible to us. That is why so many mystical experiences occur in sleep. Notice that in the Bible, many revelations and messages from God occur in sleep. Remember the story of Jacob's ladder: "And he dreamed, and behold a ladder set up on the earth, and the top of it reached to heaven: and behold the angels of God ascending and descending on it."[3]

The attainment of this magic power also happens in the clairvoyant state wherein the person does not see, hear, or feel with the physical senses because they are superseded by something greater.

It might also seem to be true that the more simple a life a person leads and the closer to nature she is, the easier it is for her spirit to liberate itself and the deeper and truer is her clairvoyant ability. Perhaps this is why the Native American Indians and other cultures that live close to nature have more insight about and more experiences of the spiritual world.

Thus in the practice of mesmerism, the suspension of the senses occurs before the clairvoyant state is reached. Initially the person becomes oblivious to the external world, and then the inner world is opened as the clairvoyant state deepens.

Kerner quotes the Seeress describing the condition that occurs when the clairvoyant state is reached:

> "From that moment, everything resolves itself into an unbounded sea of light, in which from infinite bliss I seem to be dissolved myself. Every form presents itself to me in this light—which far exceeds that of the sun—in the most defined and accurate point of view. I comprehend everything much more easily and clearly, the depths of nature are opened to me and my view of the past and the future, both as regards time and space, is like viewing the present; and are more perfect and defined in proportion to the degree of development the condition has reached."[4]

This state has been described by Jacob Böhme as the "dawn of morning rising to the center." Some people may have had glimpses of it at some time in their lives, and others may never have experienced it. It may be experienced only once in a lifetime by some; others may have many such experiences. Those who have experienced it, however, agree unanimously that words cannot describe it. These momentary experiences of this type of enlightenment are sometimes called cosmic consciousness. For most, they are fleeting, lasting only for a split second. We cannot control them; they come and go as they please. One of the first books ever written on this subject is called *Cosmic Consciousness,* by Richard Bucke, published in 1901.[5]

We continue with Kerner's description:

> Moreover, this state of sleep-waking is not so entirely liberated from its earthly shell as to be wholly free from influences; and these bright glimpses, as already observed, are often only momentary, and are

quickly obscured by clouds. Nevertheless, the veil that separates us from what is beyond, is always in some measure blown away; and we penetrate, if only with earthly and troubled eyes, and by momentary gleams, through the chinks of the coffin that encloses us, into an ocean of infinite light.[6]

Eschenmayer, a close friend of Kerner and a member of the inner circle who observed the Seeress, makes it clear that a person who experiences this clairvoyant state may not necessarily be godlike and moral. The brief glimpses into this realm may just be the result of some natural spontaneous cause. So we must be careful not to think that just because someone has a highly spiritual experience, he or she also has a high moral character and is spiritually advanced. It also could be dangerous to have these experiences before we are spiritually ready, because they can reveal the mystery of our being before we have developed the capacity to receive this higher or spiritual information.

As Kerner quotes Eschenmayer:

Persons in this condition have no merit. Whatever moral or religious ideas they may utter, they are no substantial possession; they are only the natural results of a soul freed from the load of intellectual life. And thence these persons, on awaking, resume their former situation as representatives of individual existence, altogether unconscious of secrets that have been disclosed to them. And here lies the difference betwixt the sense of the beauty of virtue and the merit of its exercise. The mere contemplation of the idea of virtue is far from the accomplishment of what is good. Yea, my beloved, let us beware of information extorted from a clear-seer. Saint Martin pronounces it dangerous, because it frequently unveils the mystery of our being before we are prepared for it.[7]

It takes much preparation, as the mystics reveal, to advance spiritually. One notion is that drugs may help us enter and advance in the spiritual world. This is false; ascended masters tell us that drugs do the opposite. They give us a false view of the spiritual world and retard our spiritual growth. We also become dependent on them and do not try to make progress in our inner life. Thus it would appear that these short-cut methods to the spiritual world do not work and are very dangerous. The age-old, tried-and-true way is through a life of prayer and meditation. Also, do not wait until you reach old age to start on the spiritual journey. The Bible and other ancient literature stress that this is a life-long process, and it is important to start when you are young.

I believe that in our ancient past, clairvoyance was used extensively as a means to diagnose and prescribe cures for patients. Kerner states:

> There was a period in ancient times when the magnetic condition was known, and where the diligent application of its operations was used as a remedy, as well as for religious and political purposes, especially by means of the laurel and of vapors; (It is to be noted, that a magnet-stone, a sort of red ochre, was generally employed for these purposes) and it was then confined to the temples of the gods as a mystery; not flung to the multitude, nor permitted to be handled by unbelievers, deriders, nor dissemblers.[8]

One example of such a place where this may have been practiced is ancient Egypt. Some Egyptologists think that some of the temples and pyramids were used for the purpose of healing and possibly for entering the spiritual realm. I believe that the ancient Egyptian religious writings (the oldest in the world), like the Pyramid Texts and the Book of the Dead, were manuals for entering into this realm.[9]

Kerner was familiar with the history of Egypt: "The sleeper was dealt with in a chamber of the temple, in solemn stillness, and generally in the night. When he awoke, the priests told him of the means he had revealed, and the result."[10]

Kerner's statement is extremely interesting since, as mentioned earlier, the Great Pyramid may have been used to stimulate paranormal experiences. In what is approximately the center of the pyramid is the King's Chamber, in which lies an empty coffin or coffer. The initiate would lie down in the empty coffin, and perhaps this produced an altered state of consciousness, or the out-of-body experience that many claimed to have experienced. The pyramid, especially the King's Chamber, is known to resonate with sound. Apparently, it was built for the purpose of sound vibration, and perhaps it was this that produced the altered state in the person. Another interesting observation is that the radioactivity level in the King's Chamber is above normal, and the presence of radioactivity does seem to stimulate paranormal or out-of-body experiences. Areas where ancient megaliths are found also seem to have an above-average level of radioactivity.[11]

Unfortunately, the person in our society who exhibits clairvoyant ability is sometimes treated as odd and may even be abused and experimented with by scientists. This happened to Edgar Cayce, who was examined by Dr. William Sadler, a well-known medical doctor from Chicago. While Cayce was in trance, Sadler stuck a long needle into his arm to see if he would react. When nothing happened, he then drove the needle into the sole of Cayce's foot. Another doctor drove a hatpin through Cayce's cheek, and another stuck a knife under the nail of one of his fingers and lifted the nail up from the flesh. Cayce didn't react to any of this and no blood flowed from any of these wounds. Afterward, the wound marks were evident, and he suffered much from them.[12] It is unfortunate that things like this happen in the name of science.

This inner life exists in all of us, in you and in me. It's part of our original being, and I consider it very unfortunate that most people don't make any effort to cultivate it. Maybe it's time for us to wake up and start to be aware of our inner life, our true nature. I believe it's humanity's destiny to awaken this clairvoyant ability, and maybe this will usher in the new age. The following words by Kerner are excellent for reflection and meditation:

And may the following pages, dear reader, which contain many strange revelations respecting the inner life, and the diffusion of a world of spirits amongst us, make clear to you that this inner life exists in us all, and at all times, and not only in the state of sleep-waking [clairvoyance]. But we do not welcome it, nor look within to seek it, nor listen to its whispers, nor trouble ourselves to discover their interpretation; because the voices from without cry ever in our ears till that moment comes—and oh! how quickly comes it to all—when the external world fades from us; and then, but too late, our spirit reverts to its inner sphere, and beholds, for the first time, the unsuspected terrors that await it.[13]

Regarding the similarity between the clairvoyant state and death, the Seeress said the separation of the spirit from the soul and the body when in the clairvoyant state bears a great resemblance to death but is not the same. In death, the spirit leaves the body completely. It's interesting to note the Seeress's and Andrew Jackson Davis's similar descriptions of death. They both said that in death, when the spirit leaves the body, the dying person is unconscious of all that happens. And while it may sometimes appear that in a dying person's last moments he is in agony, this is only the struggle of the spirit leaving the body, a struggle that produces reflexes in the body.

The Seeress's practice of continually entering into the clairvoyant state depleted her energy and contributed to her weakened condition. To sustain herself, she drew energy from other people, which she claimed did not cause any adverse effects in them, although some claimed that they experienced an ill effect.

Kerner explains:

In this state she had no organic strength, but depended wholly on that of other people, which she received chiefly through the eyes and the ends of the fingers. She said that she drew her life wholly from the air, and the nervous emanations of others, by which they lost nothing; but it is not superfluous to mention, that many persons said that they did lose strength by being long in proximity to her,

A DEATH SCENE.

Fig. 5.1. The spirit leaving the body, drawn according to Andrew Jackson Davis. Image from *Beyond the Valley*, by Andrew Jackson Davis.

and that they felt a contraction in the limbs, a tremor, etc. Many persons also, when near her, were sensible of a weakness in the eyes and at the pit of the stomach, even to fainting; and she admitted that she gained most strength from the eyes of powerful men.

From her own relations she extracted more vigor than from others; and, as she grew weaker, from them only she derived benefit. By the proximity of weak and sickly people, she grew weaker, just as flowers lose their beauty, and perish, under the same circumstances. She also drew nourishment from the air, and, even in the coldest weather, could not live without an open window.[14]

This statement about the ends of the fingers is very interesting since Kirlian photography, which claims to be able to photograph auras of living things, shows jets of energy coming out of human fingertips. Also, what spiritual or subtle substance is she extracting from the air for nourishment? Unfortunately, she did not give us any more information about this, and we can only speculate.

In addition to Frederika's psychic gift of being sensitive to the spiritual essence of people, she was, as we have mentioned, sensitive to metals, plants, and animals. Different substances produced different effects on her; she was even sensitive to electrical forces. She was also sensitive to human writing in that she could merely hold a letter and, without looking at it, know what it was about. She had an incredible number of psychic sensibilities. Many psychics have a sensitivity in only one or two areas, but she had them in great number. It must have been amazing to be in her presence.

As Dr. Kerner wrote, "From her eyes there shone a really spiritual light, of which everyone who saw her became immediately sensible; and, whilst in this state, she was more a spirit than a being of mortal mould. Should we compare her to a human being, we should rather say that she was in the state of one who, hovering between life and death, belonged rather to the world he was about to visit, than the one he was going to leave."[15]

She frequently described a state in which she could perceive her own spirit out of her body, which seemed to hover over it. When these out-of-body experiences happened to her, she described the feeling as being weightless. It is interesting to note that many times when in her clairvoyant state, she would speak in verse. She had never been trained in this, however, and never spoke in verse before doing so while in a trance state.

She was very patient and kind with everyone who came to see her. As noted, some people came to her for help and some came out of curiosity. Some even came to find ways to slander her. What she would say about those who came to her with not the best of intentions was "They have power over my body, but not over my mind."[16] She even defended those who slandered her; she was never judgmental. The sincere person who visited her came away happy with a new conviction of a future life.

Those fortunate enough to see her described her as follows: "Her fragile body enveloped her spirit, but as a gauzy veil. She was small— her features were oriental—her eyes piercing and prophetic; and their expression was heightened by her long dark eyelashes. She was a delicate flower, and lived upon sunbeams."[17]

6

SPIRIT SEEING

In nineteenth-century England and America, it was common for mediums to converse with spirits through raps (tapping), alphabet boards, trumpets, and other instruments. The Seeress, however, had no need of these, since she conversed directly with the spirits. Kerner observed that she spent more time in the spiritual world than in the physical and that her life hung to the physical world by a thread.[1] He said that "she was more than half a spirit and belonged more to a world of spirits."[2] It is important to note that she was eventually able to communicate with spirits both in her clairvoyant state and in her normal state of consciousness. Many of the spirits that came to her asked her to pray for them so that they could be released from their lower state and move on to a higher realm. She described some of the spirits that came to her as very black or gray. Moral purity or impurity, she said, is as real and as conspicuous in spirits as a dirty or clear complexion is in human beings. The ones she helped eventually became clearer, whiter, and brighter and eventually left for a higher sphere.

She explained that it was always with her own inner spiritual eye, not with the eye of the flesh, that she saw things of the spirit. She would see visions in things such as soap bubbles, glass, and mirrors. Like most clairvoyants, she could read from closed books without looking at them, see people and objects at a distance, and have glimpses of the future.

In the following passage she describes her ability to see ghosts:

I see them at various times by day and night, whether I am alone or in company. I am perfectly awake at the time, and am not sensible of any circumstance or sensation that calls them up. . . . Not that they are always with me, but they come at their own pleasure, like mortal visitors, and equally, whether I am in a spiritual or corporeal state at the time. . . . I observe frequently that when a ghost visits me by night, those who sleep in the same room with me are, by their dreams, made aware of its presence; they speak afterwards of the apparition they saw in their dream, although I have not breathed a syllable on the subject to them. . . . I feel in a sort of magnetic rapport with them. They appear to me like a thin cloud that one could see through—which, however, I cannot do. I never observed that they threw any shadow. I see them more clearly by the sun or moonlight than in the dark; but whether I could see them in absolute darkness, I do not know. If any object comes between me and them, they are hidden from me. I cannot see them with closed eyes, nor when I turn my face from them; but I am so sensible of their presence, that I could designate the exact spot which they are standing; and I can hear them speak, though I stop my ears. I cannot endure that they should approach me very near; they give me a feeling of debility. Other persons who do not see them are frequently sensible of the effects of their proximity when they are with me; they have a disposition to faintness, and feel a consriction of the nerves; even animals are not exempt from this effect. The appearance of the ghosts is the same as when they were alive, but colorless—rather grayish; so is their attire—like a cloud. The brighter and happier spirits are differently clothed; they have a long, loose, shining robe, with a girdle round the waist.

The features of the specters [ghosts] are as when alive; but mostly sad and gloomy. Their eyes are bright—often like flame. I have never seen any with hair. All the female ghosts have the same head covering—even when over it, as is sometimes the case, they have that they wore when alive. This consists of a sort of veil, which comes over the forehead, and covers the hair. The forms of the good spirits appear bright, those of the evil, dusky.

Whether it is only under this form that my senses can perceive them, and whether, to a more spiritualized being, they would not appear as spirits, I cannot say; but I suspect it. Their gait is like the gait of the living, only that the better spirits seem to float, and the evil ones tread more heavily; so that their footsteps may sometimes be heard, not by me alone, but by those who are with me.

They have various ways of attracting attention by other sounds besides speech. . . . These sounds consist of sighing, knocking, noises as of the throwing of sand or gravel, rustling of paper, rolling of a ball, shuffling as in slippers, etc. They are also able to move heavy articles, and to open and shut doors; although they can pass through these unopened, or through the walls. I observe that the darker a spectre is, the stronger is his voice, and the more ghostly power of making noises, and so forth, he seems to have. . . . They move their mouths in speaking, and their voices are as various, as those of the living. They cannot answer me all that I desire; wicked spirits are more willing or able to do this, but I avoid conversing with them. These I can dismiss by a written word, used as an amulet. . . .

When I talk to them piously, I have seen the spirits, especially the darker ones, draw in my words, as it were, whereby they become brighter; but I feel much weaker. The spirits of the happy invigorate me, and give me a very different feeling. . . . I observe that the happy spirits have the same difficulty in answering questions regarding earthly matters, as the evil ones have it, with respect to heavenly ones. The first belong not to earth, nor the last to heaven.

With the high and blessed spirits I am not in a condition to converse: I can only venture on a short interrogation. . . . When soul and spirit are united, I cannot converse with the blessed. The spirits who come to me are mostly on the inferior steps of the mid-region, which is in our atmosphere. . . . They are chiefly spirits of those who from the attraction of, and attachment to, the external world, have remained below; or of those who have not believed in their redemption through Christ, or who, in the moment of dying, have been troubled with an earthly thought which has clung to them, and impeded their upward flight. Many, who are neither condemned nor placed amongst the blessed immediately after death, are on different stages of this mid-region; some, whose spirits have been purified, are very high. On the lowest degree, these spirits are still exposed to the temptation of the wicked; but not in the higher, where they already enjoy heavenly happiness and the purity of the blessed. . . .

Those on the lower degree, who are the heaviest, are in a continual twilight, with nothing to delight their eyes. . . . It is only by their inward improvement that they obtain light and the power of seeing. As soon as they have light in their souls, they can quit our atmosphere, and they can see light again. These are they who mostly come to me. . . . They come to me that I may aid them through prayer, and give them a word of consolation. Others come under the erroneous persuasion, that the avowal of some crime which weighs upon their spirit will bring them rest. Under the influence of this error, they are often more anxious about some single misdeed than about all the rest of their ill-spent lives; and others come to me to whom some earthly feeling or thought has clung in death which they cannot shake off. It were better they addressed themselves to the Spirits of the Blessed; but their weight draws them more to men than to spirits. They come to me, and I see them independently of my own will.[3]

On being asked whether humankind could release spirits, she answered:

No; they must release themselves from the bonds that hold them. They seek help from living men; and have the idea that we can help them, because they have no comprehension of the Great Redeemer.

We can only be mediators, as I am. I always seek to persuade them from their error, that I or others can help them. I pray earnestly with them, and wean them more and more from the world; but it costs much labor before such souls are turned to the Lord. . . . There are many instances in which the half-unblessed—those in a middle stage—could raise themselves higher, since it depends on themselves to frequent good spirits and be instructed by them, when their progress would then be much faster than by the assistance of mortals.[4]

It is interesting that she says lower or evil spirits have difficulty in answering questions regarding heavenly matters. It seems to be important to know which type of spirit someone is communicating with. The higher spirits of heaven would, of course, be more reliable and truthful than a lower spirit, so we must carefully discern spirits. She even points out that wicked spirits were very anxious to help out and give information, whereas the higher spirits were more reluctant. This is important to know, since many people today think that all information from the spirit world is true and accurate.

As the Bible and other holy books tell us, test all spirits. Use your reason, judgment, and intuition and do not accept any type of spiritual communication without a thorough evaluation. Even the most well-known mystical saint, Saint Teresa of Avila, questioned her raptures and visions of God and was never 100 percent sure that they came from God. She wanted to make sure she was not being deceived, and we need to do the same thing. Many times, a spiritual director is helpful, but he or she must be knowledgeable and have experience in the metaphysical realm, or the knowledge is merely book knowledge. Too many people are willing to give advice that is not based on spiritual experience and wisdom, so be careful of what advice you accept.

Dr. Kerner makes it clear that Frederika was not the only one with the psychic ability to see spirits and be able to enter higher spiritual realms. Many others have had this gift in the past, but many have had it only partially, so their revelations were not always as accurate as hers.

He believed that the Seeress's clairvoyant ability was at a very high level, and therefore her accuracy was much greater than that of other known clairvoyants: "Her story is not to be confounded with those of persons who have only been subject to the early and imperfect magnetic conditions, and still less with those of impostors."[5]

Many mediums have partial or limited psychic ability, and the messages and information they receive is imperfect and distorted. This is what is referred to as "imperfect magnetic conditions." The more perfect and highly advanced a seer or seeress is, the more accurate is the information he or she obtains from the spiritual world. It may be like looking through frosted glass. The less frosted and clearer the glass, the more accurately one can see the world.

Now, if the more perfect mediums are tapping in to the same higher source for information, why do their descriptions concerning their revelations of the higher spheres sometimes vary? If there is only one higher reality, you would expect the same description of it from all of them. The truth, after all, is the truth, and it is timeless. When you look closely at some acknowledged seers, such as Galen, Swedenborg, Plato, and Davis, it is astounding that much of what they say is, in fact, similar. The details may differ, but the general message seems to be the same. As well, remember that they are also not immune to filtering this information through their body, and thus there may be slight differences in each of their levels of clairvoyance. There is also the problem of individual interpretation of higher knowledge. And what about imposters? Kerner writes: "The existence of one genuine pearl cannot be disproved by the production of a thousand false ones."[6]

The Seeress was no imposter. One imposter, or even many, does not invalidate a real phenomenon. Unfortunately, when imposters are exposed, many people then reject the entire phenomenon and assume everyone is a fake. Also, it is interesting to note that some seers who had the real gift could not always control it and produce this ability at will. When they were under pressure to perform, they would sometimes rely upon tricks. When exposed, they were labeled as charlatans, even though many of their mediumship experiences in the past had, in fact, been real.

Another question that often comes up is, Where is the information coming from? What is its source? Do clairvoyants have access to a higher spiritual reality or are they getting it from the mind of another individual, through something like ESP? Obviously, it's important to validate that the information comes from higher spiritual sources and not other individuals.

In the 1800s a common claim against psychics, seers, and clairvoyants was that there was an Odylic force* that people gave off, and the medium could get information from this. A very interesting and rare book that discusses this idea is *Modern Mysteries Explained and Exposed* (1855).[7] It asserts that when mediums or seers claim to contact a spirit, it is not really the spirit they are getting the information from, but that person's or another's own conscious or subconscious mind via this subtle Odylic force. What is interesting, however, is that in admitting to some unknown and unidentified spiritual Odylic force, they are admitting to something that is just as paranormal as is contact with a spirit.

This accusation was also made of Andrew Jackson Davis, even though he accurately predicted scientific discoveries of the century subsequent to his and produced information not known to any living person at that time. Some claimed that his scribe, William Fishbough, was the source of the conveyed information. It was Davis's subconscious connection with Fishbough, and not the higher spheres, that some thought Davis was tapping in to. With regard to the Seeress, the way to prove or disprove that the information came to her from the Odylic force was to show that the information she obtained was beyond what

---

*In the nineteenth century, the Odylic force was considered to be an unknown, ethereal, biological force or vital energy existing throughout the universe. The term was coined in 1845 by Baron Karl von Reichenbach. The Odylic force was useful in explaining the phenomena of mesmerism and hypnotism. Today, some think it is the same force that is known as *prana,* or *chi.*

any living person would have known. In her case, her predictions, inner language, and diagnoses and cures could have come not from any living person but only from a higher sphere or plane.

As Kerner says:

> It has been frequently asserted that the extraordinary magnetic condition of the Seeress is to be ascribed to the influence of others. How can we answer such an absurd objection? To those who followed and observed throughout the course of these phenomena, the assertion is not only false but ridiculous.
>
> Neither are her Revelations to be judged as if they were portions of a system of philosophy constructed by an enlightened mind; they are revelations drawn from the intimate contemplation of nature herself, and will therefore frequently be found not only in strict conformity with popular belief, but also with the opinions of Plato, both of which sprung from the same source.[8]

Kerner wonders why the learned were so upset with and opposed to the Seeress. What were they so afraid of? "It is certainly hard," he said, "and we cannot wonder at the annoyance it occasions, that a weak silly woman should thus disturb the established systems of the learned, and revive persuasions that it has long been the aim of the wise amongst men to eradicate."[9] This also happens today with any new or alternative view that challenges the standard academic view or academic party line. Professors are afraid of not getting tenure, for instance, if they discover or propose something radically different from their colleagues' traditional point of view. This ridiculing of new ideas is a weapon that is just as effective today as it has been throughout history.

The Seeress described the different spiritual states one can obtain and divided them into four ascending degrees.

First degree. In this state one appears to be in an ordinary, normal awake state, but actually is not. This was the first stage of the opening of their inner life. She said that many people are in this state, but they are unaware of it.

Second degree. This state she called the magnetic dream. She believed that many individuals who were in this state were considered insane. The inner world is starting to open up to them, and they may start to experience strange phenomena that they cannot explain.

Third degree. She called this state the half-waking state. In this state she could write and speak in the inner language of the spirits.

Fourth degree. This last state is the pure clairvoyant or what she called the sleep-waking state. In this state she was able to diagnose, prescribe, and have glimpses of the future.

She said that this clairvoyant or sleep-waking state contains proof of a future existence and a reunion with deceased loved ones after death.

Kerner gives an excellent definition of clairvoyance: "Clairvoyance is a state of the most perfect vigilance, because then the inner spiritual man is disentangled and set free from the body. I would rather therefore denominate sleep-waking the coming forward of the inner-man, or the spiritual growth of man. At these moments the spirit is quite free and able to separate itself from the soul and body, and go where it will, like a flash of lightning."[10]

7

SPIRITUALISM

S*piritualism* is a word one doesn't often hear today. It's been replaced with its modern equivalent: channeling. There are television programs, books, workshops, and lectures on this subject. There even are 900 numbers you can call to have someone channel information for you from an ancient spirit, for a price. One of the most famous channelers is John Edwards, who has his own television show. Thus, today spiritualism is alive and well, albeit with a new name.

The terms *clairvoyant, mystic, seeress,* and even *psychic* were used to define the abilities of the Seeress. It would be very appropriate and fitting if we also called her a spiritualist or a channeler, since she meets all the criteria of this description. Since this is the case, I thought it would be important to discuss spiritualism, its history, and some interesting historical examples of it.

The origins of spiritualism are as old as humankind itself. Early humans believed that somehow the deceased survived after death and could come back to either haunt them or help them. Depending on the circumstance, the spirit and its appearance could be positive or negative. Thus we have good spirits and bad spirits. This early belief was why the dead were buried. It was thought that by placing the body of the deceased deep in the ground, its spirit or essence would not come back to bother or haunt anyone.

As time went on, humans developed more-sophisticated ideas about death and what happened to the spirit when one's life was over. Belief in the existence of spirits and their ability to come back and affect us is found in the earliest cultures, including the Egyptians, Sumerians, and Babylonians. The Greeks, for example, utilized oracles to communicate with the dead and their gods. Native American Indians also believed that they could contact the spirits of the dead. In the Bible, the first mention of spirit communication is in the book of Samuel, when Saul tries to contact the Witch of Endor.[1]

In more recent times, we have only to look to the experiences of Emanuel Swedenborg (1688–1772) to corroborate this belief system. Swedenborg was a Swedish scientist, philosopher, and astronomer who, at the age of fifty-six, claimed to be able to contact spirits when he was in a trance state. They taught him the mysteries of the afterlife and described the spirit worlds to him. According to Swedenborg, the spirit world was made up of spheres; spirits would progress and move from one sphere to another as they developed.

The main event usually considered the catalyst of the modern or American spiritualist movement in the United States occurred in 1848. At this time, two little girls (the Fox sisters, thirteen-year-old Maggie and eleven-year-old Kate) began to hear rapping sounds in their home in Hydesville, New York. Initial investigation ruled out that the girls were producing these sounds themselves, and it was suspected they were produced by spirits trying to communicate with them. The spirits used these rapping sounds as a means of establishing a dialogue. It appeared that these sisters had mediumistic powers and were communicating with a person named Charles Rosna, who told them he had been killed and was buried in the basement of their house. In later years, debunkers claimed that the Fox sisters themselves had made the sounds. However, many years later, bones were found in the basement. Horace Greeley, then the editor of the *New York Tribune,* witnessed the sisters' rapping for himself and believed the phenomenon was genuine. He even became one of their sponsors and shared his home with them during their visits to New York City.

In 1888 (forty years later), Maggie claimed that she and her sister had faked the sounds. The following year, however, Maggie recanted her confession and said she had made the statements because she was under the sway of enemies of the spiritualist movement and also under financial pressure. Many believe that there is no concrete evidence that the Fox sisters faked the rapping sounds. Thus the debate goes on.

In this manner the American spiritualist movement started, and people from all over the United States began experimenting with the phenomenon. It was the new craze to be a spiritualist, and a séance (French for "session") was the most popular event one could attend. At a typical séance, many different methods could be employed to communicate with spirits. For instance, the spirits could speak through trumpets, materialize in a physical form, levitate tables and other objects, and/or produce automatic writing. Spiritualistic churches sprang up all over the country, and the rage was on.

A very interesting side aspect of the American spiritualist movement is whether Abraham Lincoln was involved in it. I bring this up since there has been a great interest in Lincoln and his spiritual views because of his bicentennial anniversary coming up in 2009. It is well known and documented that Lincoln's wife, Mary Todd Lincoln, was very interested in spiritualism and attended many séances. In fact, séances were held at the White House and at the Lincolns' summer residence at the Soldiers Home (also in Washington, D.C.). The Red Room in the White House was originally called the Séance Room. Lincoln attended several séances, which I have documented from original source material.[2]

In 1862 Abraham Lincoln attended his first séance, which took place at the White House with a sixteen-year-old girl named Nettie Colburn Maynard, a well-respected medium of the day. Many famous individuals attended her séances. They included Joshua Speed, who was Lincoln's close personal friend, as well as prominent congressmen Rufus R. Dawes of Maine, D. E. Somes of Massachusetts, and John Farnsworth of Illinois. Horace Greeley was also very interested in spiritualism and helped spread its influence, as did William Lloyd Garrison, the famous abolitionist; James Fenimore Cooper; and William Cullen Bryant.

Nettie Colburn Maynard published an account of this 1862 séance, as did another witness to it, by the name of Colonel S. P. Kase.[3] This is an excerpt from Nettie's description of that first meeting with Lincoln and the séance that ensued:

> He [Lincoln] stood before me, tall and kindly, with a smile on his face. . . . While he was yet speaking, I lost all consciousness of my surroundings and passed under control. For more than an hour I was made to talk to him, and I learned from my friends afterward that it was upon matters that he seemed to fully understand, while they comprehended very little until that portion was reached that related to the forthcoming Emancipation Proclamation. He was charged with the utmost solemnity and force of manner not to abate the terms of its issue, and not to delay its enforcement as a law beyond the opening of the year; and he was assured that it was to be the crowning event of his administration and life; and that while he was counseled by strong parties to defer enforcement of it, hoping to supplant it by other measures and to delay action, he must in no wise heed such counsel, but stand firm to his convictions and fearlessly perform the work and fulfill the mission for which he had been raised up by an overruling Providence. . . . Mr. Somes said, "Mr. President, would it be improper for me to inquire whether there has been any pressure brought to bear upon you to defer the enforcement of the Proclamation?" To which the President replied: "Under these circumstances that question is perfectly proper, as we are all friends. It is taking all my nerve and strength to withstand such a pressure."[4]

Arthur Conan Doyle, who was a psychic researcher and the creator of Sherlock Holmes, said that this meeting between Lincoln and Nettie was one of the most important events in the history of the United

States and that this spirit message strengthened the president in taking a difficult step to which he was not yet firmly committed.

So, did spiritualism change the face of this nation? Is it possible that without the reinforcement of the information that Lincoln received from this séance he would not have issued the Emancipation Proclamation? I don't believe this was the case, but it's certainly a very interesting event in the history of our nation and demonstrates the influence of spiritualism at that time.

The last documented séance that Lincoln attended was in 1864. Lincoln asked Congressman Somes to bring Nettie Colburn Maynard to the White House for a secret session. Lincoln told Somes to "consider the matter confidential." At the scheduled time, Somes and Nettie were brought upstairs to the executive chamber, where the president and two other gentlemen were waiting. This is the description of the event by Nettie:

> We sat quiet for a few moments before I became entranced. One hour later I became conscious of my surroundings, and was standing by a long table, upon which was a large map of the Southern States. In my hand was a lead pencil, and the tall man, with Mr. Lincoln, was standing beside me, bending over the map, while the younger man was standing on the other side of the table, looking curiously and intently at me. Somewhat embarrassed, I glanced around to note Mrs. Lincoln quietly conversing in another part of the room. The only remarks I heard were these: "It is astonishing," said Mr. Lincoln, "how every line she has drawn conforms to the plan agreed upon." "Yes," answered the older soldier, "it is very astonishing." Looking up, they both saw that I was awake, and they instantly stepped back, while Mr. Lincoln took the pencil from my hand and placed a chair for me. . . . Shortly afterwards, when about leaving, Mr. Lincoln said to us in a low voice, "It is best not to mention this meeting at present." Assuring him of silence upon the question, we were soon again on our way.[5]

MRS. NETTIE COLBURN MAYNARD.
Photographed from miniature, 1863.

Fig. 7.1. Nettie Colburn Maynard (1863). This image is from *Was Abraham Lincoln a Spiritualist?* by Nettie Colburn Maynard.

I think historians downplay Lincoln's involvement in spiritualism because they themselves do not believe in its authenticity. Lincoln not only attended séances, but actually, as in the case above, arranged one. Did spiritualism really help him issue the Emancipation Proclamation? We probably will never know the answer to this for certain, but if it did, this could be the most important event involving spiritualism in our nation's history. In my opinion, the most compelling evidence of Lincoln's belief in spiritualism is this séance that he arranged with his military officers in which Nettie gave them information by pointing to a military map on the table. Here, the commander in chief and top military leaders were getting military advice from an eighteen-year-old medium.

You must realize that all the events that I have described, from those of the Fox sisters to Abraham Lincoln's séances, happened *after* the death of the Seeress. She was one of the first clairvoyants in modern times to be an actual spiritualist. She was able to communicate with spirits freely; most of the phenomena associated with modern spiritualism originated with her. She is one of the least acknowledged and recognized spiritualists of the nineteenth century and, in my opinion, one of the most important ones.

Among other well-known spiritualists of the 1800s were Cora Richmond, Emma Harding Britten, and psychic investigators like Arthur Conan Doyle and Sir William Crookes. Spiritualism eventually started to die down, and by the end of the nineteenth century and into the early twentieth, there were few spiritualist churches or acknowledged spiritualists.

Psychometry is another aspect of spiritualism that you may have witnessed on some psychic-detective television shows. In this practice, a psychic is given a piece of clothing from a missing person and tries to identify the missing person's location. In many cases he or she is accurate and is able to help the police locate the individual, or, unfortunately, in many cases, the remains.

Psychometry is defined as the reading of objects by touch and generally refers to the ability to gain impressions and information about an object, or anything connected to it, by holding it in one's hand. A person with this ability is called a psychometrist. This term was first coined in 1842 by Joseph R. Buchanan, an American physiologist who claimed that psychometry could be used to measure the "soul of all things." Buchanan further said that the past is entombed in the present.

The Seeress had this psychometric ability also. She could sense information from merely holding a person's hand or an object. This is how Andrew Jackson Davis, in his later years as a physician, would diagnose his patients.[6] He would place the patient's hand in his palm and thereby be able to determine his or her exact illness and know what to prescribe for its cure. Edgar Cayce also had this gift. It's interesting to note the many similarities in the process of diagnosing and prescribing among true clairvoyants.

I have an interesting personal story about psychometry. Several years ago, I had the opportunity to obtain an extremely rare and unique Lincoln relic, a piece of old lace that appears to have bloodstains on it. The relic came with an old note reading: "Lincoln's Bloodstained cloth from April 15, 1865, presented by Doctor Leale of N.Y." Its provenance can be traced back to the estate of one of Lincoln's private secretaries, a man by the name of John Hay. At one point Dr. Robert White, the famous Kennedy collector, was the relic's owner, before it changed hands again. I didn't know where the lace came from, what kind of fabric it was originally part of, or how the bloodstains were caused. The note was all I had to go on at that time.

Dr. Charles Leale was an Army physician from New York and was the first physician to attend Lincoln after he'd been shot in Ford's Theatre. I have interviewed Dr. Leale's granddaughter Helen Harper Leale.[7] We're not sure of the lace's origins. It may have been from a dress belonging to either Mary Todd Lincoln or an actress at Ford's Theatre by the name of Laura Keene, who held Lincoln's bleeding head that night. It might be a piece of clothing, a bedsheet or pillow from the bed in the Peterson House, in which Lincoln died, or a handkerchief that his head was placed on in Ford's Theatre after he was shot.

After a year of extensive research with Lincoln historians from all over the country—library curators, the supervisor at Ford's Theatre,[8] individuals associated with Ford's Theatre in Washington as well as learned individuals at the Lincoln Presidential Library, the Illinois Historical Society, the Lace Museum in California, and the John Hay Library (among other places)—I decided to try something different. A good friend of mine who is a semiretired medical doctor told me

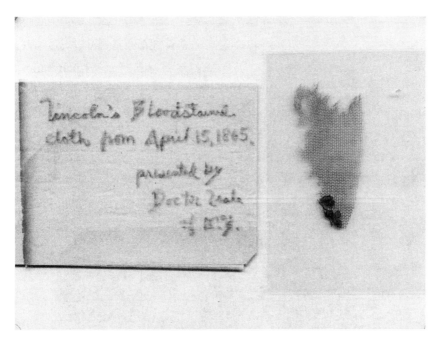

Fig. 7.2. A handwritten note (left) pertaining to the piece of lace from Ford's Theatre (right). The lace measures two and a half inches by one inch, with an embroidery pattern and bloodstains on it. Photograph by John DeSalvo.

that a close friend of his, an engineer by profession, was also a gifted psychometrist. He arranged a lunch meeting for the three of us, and I brought along the relic.

The psychometrist held the relic and said that it was authentic and did have on it the actual blood of Lincoln. I then asked him if he knew where the lace had come from. He said that it had been used like a cheesecloth (gauze) by the doctors to try to stop the bleeding on Lincoln's head. He explained it came from a curtain. This would be consistent with everything I knew about the relic and the facts associated with the assassination.

Additional research seemed to substantiate this. The day after the assassination, photographs had been taken of Lincoln's theater booth. There were two booths next to each other, and Lincoln had occupied the one on the right. I noticed that there was a fine linen curtain in the booth on the left but not in the one on the right. I had never noticed this before, even after having looked at this photo many times previously. Unfortunately, we have nothing to compare my linen sample with. The curtains disappeared right after the assassination; they were cut up and taken by relic hunters (which is another indication that my scrap was part of that curtain from the booth on the right).

My next step was to contact the person responsible for the reconstruction project of Ford's Theatre many years ago, who still owned an

Fig. 7.3. Brady photograph of the president's box. Image from the National Archives and Records Administration.

embroidery company located in western New York. His name is Vincent Mesiano, and he is a tremendous and kind person. Vincent sent me a sample of the curtain he reconstructed based on the Brady photograph. This sample had an embroidery pattern on it that exactly resembled my piece of lace. He had reconstructed the curtains based on photos taken at Ford's Theatre at the time of the assassination and supplied to him by the National Archives.

If you compare the reconstruction sample (figure 7.4) with my relic (figure 7.5), you can see the remarkable similarities. Note that the embroidery pattern of the three-petaled flower and stem is virtually identical on both samples.

Thus psychometry helped verify an important part of my Lincoln research. I believe I am the only person to own a piece of the original Ford's Theatre curtain that has Lincoln's blood on it. I hope to have it displayed at Ford's Theatre to illustrate the research process of this relic.

Today we have many interesting applications of psychometry, and many people believe in the validity of these phenomena. We have to acknowledge the Seeress as one of the first in modern times to practice this mysterious art.

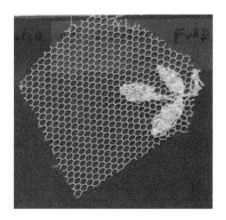
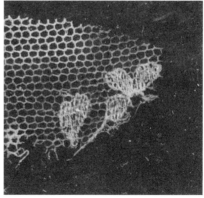

Fig. 7.4. Linen reconstructed by Vincent Mesiano from the Brady photograph. Photograph by John DeSalvo.

Fig. 7.5. Close-up of embroidered pattern of the actual relic. Photograph by John DeSalvo.

8

DEVELOPMENT
OF THE INNER LIFE

The Seeress has some important things to say considering the spiritual life and how we should give this top priority in our lives. Her thoughts on this are excellent for meditation and reflection: "As must every man who, isolating himself from the hurry and bustle of external life, to contemplate his inner self, you will feel, dear reader, that our inner and outer life are not only different, but often in flat contradiction of each other."[1]

The first part of what she says above is so important for our individual spiritual development. In the Carmelite order, which was founded by St. Teresa of Avila, contemplation is the most important aspect of the community.[2] Many Eastern disciplines also focus on meditation and mental prayer. Everyone should set some time apart every day for meditation, or just inner quietude. This helps reduce and block out the noise in our minds and allows us to go within ourselves and experience our true nature in order to be present with God.

It's also true that our inner and outer lives are always in contradiction or conflict with each other. The constant battle between the spirit and the flesh goes on every day; we are always trying to decide whether to make the correct moral choice versus the self-interested, earthly decision. It is important for us to be able to distinguish between the higher and lower selves. It appears that as we advance spiritually, we become more in tune with making the right spiritual decision over the earthly decision. As we become more unified with our spiritual nature, we open ourselves to the voice of God.

As Kerner stated, "What the outer life finds decorous, the inner frequently condemns; and in the midst of the world we are often disquieted by a still small voice that whispers us from within."[3] This "still small voice" is referred to in I Kings 19:11–13. The Lord appears to Elijah as "a gentle whisper." The Lord tells him to go stand on the mountain, for He is about to pass by. First a great wind tears apart the mountains and shatters the rocks, but the Lord is not in the wind. Then an earthquake occurs, but the Lord is not in the earthquake. After that a fire comes, but the Lord is not in the fire. Finally, there is a gentle whisper. That is when Elijah pulls his cloak over his face in humility and realizes that the presence of God is in that gentle whisper.

This biblical story is very revealing, in that we tend to look for God in all the wrong places. God may not talk to us in a thundering voice or an apparition, but it is that small voice within us by which we communicate with God. This practice is like trying to tune in a radio station. As we fine-tune the dial, the station becomes clearer. That is what we need to do. We need to fine-tune our listening so we can hear that small voice within.

It's interesting that the Seeress agrees with many religions in believing that we are held accountable for our thoughts, words, and deeds during our lifetime, and we must face them in the afterlife: "Every act and thought, however trifling it may now appear, is . . . noted and numbered; and will one day or other appear in bright relief before our spiritual eyes, when our bodily ones are forever extinguished."[4]

This concept is very common in many religions and spiritual beliefs. Others refer to a karmic record in which all thoughts, words, and deeds are recorded. Thus we will have to answer for everything we have done in this world. This is a sobering thought, and maybe if we truly believed it, we would lead better lives. Many people who have had a near death experience report that they relive their life in a short period of time and can see everything that they have done as if watching a motion picture. It's thought that the brain may also record everything like a phonograph record or CD. I think it's more like a holographic recording.

Thus, to be more spiritual and godlike, we must strive to reduce the noise of the outside world and listen more to our inner voice, or spiritual self. The Seeress says that we also get help from spiritual sources: "The more, in the tumult of the world and the bustle of existence, this inner life makes itself felt—the more the gentle voices within us drown the loud music of the world—the greater is our debt to the spirit that guides us (*Our protecting spirit*)."[5]

We have a choice, and when we accept the reality of our spiritual existence, we will lead better and more fulfilling lives. If not, someday we will be truly sorry for our missed opportunities:

> But if thou art carried away by the current of worldly life, seeking only what belongs to it, believe, dear reader that an hour will one day come, and God grant it be not thy last! An hour of sorrow and of tears—an hour when thou shall stand by the death-bed of thy beloved, or from the summit of earthly happiness be cast into the depths of repentance and of shame, deserted and alone—when thy inner life shall rise up before thee, embracing thee again within its sphere; that life which, since thy childhood, has been hidden from thee, of which thou hast only been visited by glimpses in thy dreams—dreams which thou knewest not to interpret.[6]

Perhaps now is the time for amending our mistakes. If we do it now, maybe we will not face reconciliation in the afterlife. Acknowledging our faults (Know thyself) and trying to make better spiritual progress are among our most important goals in this life.

It has been observed many times that just before someone dies, he or she may become aware of other spirits and/or the spiritual world. He may communicate this to others in the room, who probably think the dying person is hallucinating. The dying also speak of a deceased relative or spouse who may be present to help them make the transition to the next life. Is this just a chemical reaction of the dying brain and the release of old memories, or are those who are dying actually seeing spirits from the spiritual world that they will soon be entering? I believe the latter; spirits are not only here to help and guide us while we are alive, but they are also present during our transition to the spiritual world:

> To so many will it yet, who, now joyous and with unclouded brows, are wholly engrossed with the interests of this world, and devoting all their best faculties to their advancement! By the bedside of such a one I once stood, and, with the death-rattle in his throat, he said to me, "I feel that my life passed from my brain to the epigastric region; of my brain I have no more consciousness—I no longer feel my arms nor my feet; but I see inexpressible things—things which I never believed; there is another world!" And so saying, he expired.[7]

I want to bring up an interesting theory of mine regarding the phenomena claimed by many who have had a near death experience. I do believe that many times strange phenomena may have more than one explanation. When an individual undergoes a near death experience, often he speaks of going through a long tunnel and seeing light at the end of it. One explanation of this tunnel may be that during the death process, our first memories are brought back, and those would be of the birth process, of us coming out or descending from the womb into the physical world. This would resemble going out of a tunnel into the light. I do believe, in many cases, that this is a real spiritual experience and the person is actually seeing the spiritual light of the afterworld.

Some Christian religions talk about a Communion of Saints; essentially, this doctrine is a communication between the spiritual and physical worlds. Kerner quotes the philosopher Schelling on the death of a friend's wife. It illustrates that love is a strong bond between the different worlds:

> *Remembrance* is but a feeble expression to convey the intimate connection which exists betwixt those who are departed and those who remain. In our innermost being, we are in strict union with the dead; for in our better part we are no other than what they are—spirits. The future reunion of accordant souls, who through life have had one love, one faith, and one hope, is a thing to be confidently relied on, being one of the promises of Christianity to be faithfully fulfilled to all, however difficult the conception is, even to those minds most accustomed to abstract contemplations. I am daily more satisfied that, as we might expect, there is a mutual dependence betwixt things essentially personal and things immortal. If more were needed to confirm this persuasion in those who think and feel rightly, the death of one bound to us by the fondest ties of love, is sufficient to set on it the seal of conviction. It is when we know that life is fading from us, and that for us there is no more pleasure in the world, we first begin to live for God. Then, when the external world sinks from us, the inner life ascends. It needs no sleep-waking to perceive this inner life; to every man who is not too much entangled in the world—to him who lives in it, but is not of it—is given an eye to discern it.[8]

The last section of the last sentence is similar to the biblical expression: "He that has ears to hear, let him hear."[9] Jesus utters this expression many times in the Gospels, which means it is very significant. Do we listen to the inner voice within us?

In reading the lives of the saints and mystics of all ages and beliefs, we find that they did not ignore the world and become hermits to meditate all day long: "If we read the history of the saints," Kerner wrote, "we shall find innumerable facts bearing testimony to the power of the inner life."[10] They were very active in the world and tried to improve it and make a difference. They were the great reformers and tried to battle injustice and prejudice. They carried out all their duties and responsibilities to the best of their abilities. They did not flee to the mountaintop to escape the world. Likewise, we all have our roles to play in the world; hopefully we can make a difference. As Kerner himself writes, "But these wonders of the inner life are also known to others, who, from their youth up, have led a temperate, simple, God-given life, without despising their daily duties, but strongly and worthily fulfilling them. We are instructed also by certain significant dreams, presentiments, and communications from the world of spirits; and also from what is only to be learnt by the revelations of the magnetic life."[11]

Kerner mentions Frederika's grandfather Johann Schmidgall (whom we discussed in the introduction). Kerner describes what happened to him shortly before he died:

> One morning, as he [Johann Schmidgall] arose from his bed more cheerful than usual, he narrated to his children, that in the foregoing night, his blessed wife had appeared to him in a dream, more distinctly than anything of the sort he ever remembered. She had said something to him, but what it was he could not recall. When this happened he was in perfect health—but seven days afterwards—dead.
>
> In the same night that Schmidgall had this dream, his granddaughter [Frederika], who was far away from him, lay in sickness and suffering for twelve hours, buried in the profoundest depths of her inner life—in that condition of inner wakefulness, which is called magnetic sleep-waking; spoke to her and said, "I know not wherefore thy protecting spirit, [this was Frederika's grandmother: the wife of Schmidgall,] has for seven days abandoned thee, and is engaged with something of more importance that is occurring in thy family—and without her support thou couldst not bear with me.[12]

The chemist and alchemist Jan Baptista van Helmont is quoted by Kerner. The following statement of van Helmont is quite powerful and sums up much of what we have been discussing:

> When God created the human soul, he communicated to it essential and original knowledge. This soul is the mirror of the universe, and is in connection with all beings. She is lighted by a light from within; but the storms of passion, and the multitude of sensuous impressions, and the distractions of the world, darken this light, whose beams are only shed when it burns alone, and all within us is in peace and harmony. If we would abstract ourselves from all external influences, and follow this light alone, we should find within ourselves true and unerring counsel. In this state of concentration the soul discriminates between all objects to which its observation is directed. It can unite itself with them—penetrate their properties—and, reaching up to God, through him attain the most important truths.
>
> If we go back into the primitive ages, when men dwelt under the dominion of nature, before the inner life was stifled by what is called cultivation—in the history of the Old Testament, for example, or even now in the East, which was the cradle of mankind—we shall find remnants of this inner life exhibited by entire races of people— such as, when they are observed in individuals here, we are accustomed to look upon as symptoms of disease.[13]

Van Helmont, in my opinion, is referring to a Rosicrucian expression, "As above, so below," when he mentions that the "soul is the mirror of the universe." Early humans were more aware of the spiritual world than we are. They were closer to God and nature and may have had an ability to see into the spiritual world. It is unfortunate that we have lost this ability. How different the world would be today if humankind had retained it.

9

SPIRITUAL
SENSITIVITIES

Many psychics and clairvoyants have claimed that stones, metals, plants, animals, and people all have some subtle or spiritual essence within them. Some may call this a spirit or soul, but whatever it's called, this essence is something beyond the physical. Most individuals can't perceive this essence, and science has not been able to measure or identify it. It seems to be perceivable by those who can enter the clairvoyant state. Those who possess this sensitivity have the ability to sense the spiritual or magical properties of both inanimate and animate objects. They also seem to be able to locate and identify objects hidden underground, and they have the ability to locate underground water, a practice known as dowsing.

An interesting example of the magical properties of stones and gems comes from the Hebrew Scriptures, in which a high priest is described as wearing a breastplate studded with jewels placed over his stomach, which he used for divination. The high priest would practice divination by using something the Bible calls the Urim and the Thummim. In Exodus, it says, "And thou shalt put on the breastplate of judgment, the Urim and the Thummim; and they shall be upon Aaron's heart, when he goeth in before the Lord: and Aaron shall bear the judgment of the children of Israel upon his heart before the Lord continually."[1]

The priest would use these to cast lots. We do not know for sure what these objects were and how they were used, but many think they were two stones with writing on them; perhaps one was white and the other black, signifying yes and no. Thus, the high priest would ask a question and then pick one stone from his pocket where he kept them and read the response.

I once heard that the Urim and the Thummim were not two stones with a yes and no on them, but twenty-two stones, each one having one letter of the twenty-two letters of the Hebrew alphabet on it. Maybe by selecting the stones one after another, something would be spelled out. This is similar to how a Ouija board works. Many believe that the Hebrew alphabet is a mystical alphabet and has magical properties. This would make sense if it was a remnant from the Primal Language. Aristotle, Galen, Pliny, Hildegard of Bingen, and many others also allude to the magic power of stones, which were used as talismans and charms in their day.

Some modern mystics have claimed that these stones no longer have or carry the same properties as they did in the past—"the aspect of the heavens not being the same."[2] It is very interesting that the spiritual conditions of the heavens do not remain the same throughout history and are constantly changing. Many years ago, in the 1970s, when I took a Transcendental Meditation course, I heard this statement in reference to meditation. I was told that it is more difficult to meditate in our present, modern world than it was in the ancient world, because today there is more noise on both the spiritual and the physical planes. This noise and disturbance hinders our ability to achieve transcendence during meditation. It appears that meditation in the ancient world was more natural and effortless than it is today. Thus we can't get the same results in metaphysical exercises as the ancients did. This is good to know and may explain why many spiritual practices that worked in the past do not work now. It has also been said that even if the heavens are the same, humankind has changed. When humans were closer to nature and less entangled with noisy civilization, they were more sensitive to spiritual influences.

The Seeress had this sensitivity to inanimate objects, plants, and animals.

Dr. Kerner explains:

It is remarkable that colored stones produced much more effect upon Mrs. H. [Kerner usually refers to the Seeress as Mrs. H., i.e., Mrs. Hauffe] than those that were colorless. . . . Mrs. H., however, never looked at the minerals. The experiments were made by placing them in her hand, without telling her what they were. She was very sensible of the effects of glass and crystal; they awakened her from her somnambulic state; and if allowed to lie long on the pit of her stomach, produced catalepsy. She was affected in the same manner by sand, or even standing for some time near a glass window. The odor of sand and glass was very perceptible and very agreeable to her; but if she chanced to seat herself on a sandstone bench, she was apt to become cataleptic; and once, having been for some time missed, she was at length found at the top of the house, seated on a heap of sand, so rigid, that she had been unable to move away from it.

Our experiments with respect to the effects of minerals on Mrs. H. were confirmed in other forms—namely, by placing a divining rod, or pendulum of hazel, in her left hand, which she held over the different substances; and we then found that those which produced no effects on her had no attraction for the wand, and vice versa. These experiments might have been carried much farther—as by placing the various substances on the pit of her stomach, for example—had I not apprehended the effects on her excitable constitution.[3]

Dr. Kerner and others observed strange physical phenomena occurring around the Seeress at various times that they could not explain scientifically. For example, if she was taking a bath during her clairvoyant state, she became more buoyant than a cork. Every effort to submerge her body by her attendants failed, and she could not be kept down in the water. This was not just normal floating but a phenomenon that cannot be explained by standard means. Why this is interesting is that during the witch hunts and trials of the seventeenth century, there was a water test that was applied to suspected witches. The accused woman would be thrown in the water, and if she floated, it would prove she was a witch. If she drowned, it would prove otherwise, so it would be a no-win situation for the accused.

Other unusual sensitivities of the Seeress included being aware of a person's moral character; she said there was such a thing as *moral weight*. The physical body of a person with good moral character would appear to be light to her, even if the person was large and heavy, and a person with poor moral character would appear very heavy and large, regardless of his or her physical weight.

She was even sensitive to sunlight, which had varying physical effects on her. Even the different colors in a ray of light each had its peculiar effect. The light of the moon affected her only if she looked directly at it; this produced melancholy and a cold shiver. She was very much affected by lightning and perceived flashes that were invisible to other people. If someone touched her with his finger during an electrical storm, small flashes of light would ascend to the ceiling. If a man touched her, these flashes were colorless, and from women they were blue. She was able to perceive flashes from people's eyes, and this would tell her something about them. She could not drink rainwater that had fallen during an electrical storm on account of the heat that she sensed it contained. She was affected by any form of electricity.

She could not exist without an open window and claimed to be able to extract a vivifying principle from the air. She never identified or described what this substance was. She also said that there is another substance in the air that spirits make use of to render themselves audible and visible to mortals.

Often when a person dies, someone in the room of the dying person is inspired to open a window or door to help the spirit leave. The Seeress was of the opinion that opening a window at the moment of a person's death was not mere superstition but that it actually facilitated the release of the soul from that person. Andrew Jackson Davis and other clairvoyants said the same thing. It is not essential that a window be opened, since the spirit can pass through physical objects. However, given that it is habitual while alive to leave a building through a door, it seems that spirits tend to prefer leaving through a similar opening at the time their spirit leaves the earthly plane. It is not essential that they do this, but it does facilitate the process.[4]

When the Seeress looked directly into a person's right eye, she saw, just behind her reflected image, the image of another person. This image was not of her or of the person whose eyes she was looking into. She believed it to be the picture of that person's inner self. This internal image reflected the moral character of that person, and for some it was more beautiful and more pure than his or her physical appearance, for it reflected the purity of that person's being. Maybe that's why, when we look directly into a person's eyes, we feel that we sense the person's soul. If the Seeress looked into a person's left eye, she immediately saw whatever disease existed in that person and could prescribe a treatment for him or her.

What's interesting is that she also saw something when she looked into the eyes of animals. If she looked into the right eye of a dog or a fowl, she saw a blue flame, which to her meant that she was seeing its soul. (So perhaps animals do have souls after all!) She said that she saw these second images with her spiritual eyes and not her physical eyes. This was also how she claimed to see spirits—through her spiritual eyes. We all have spiritual eyes, but most of us do not use them or are not even aware of their existence.

Dr. Kerner describes what the Seeress could see with her spiritual eyes:

> Soap-bubbles, glass, and mirrors, excited her spiritual eye. A child happening to blow soap bubbles: She exclaimed, "Ah! My God! I behold in the bubbles every thing I think of, although it be distant—not in little, but as large as life—but it frightens me." I

then made a soap bubble, and bade her look for her child that was far away. She said she saw him in bed, and it gave her much pleasure. At another time she saw my wife, who was in another house, and described precisely the situation she was in at the moment—a point I took care immediately to ascertain. She was, however, with difficulty induced to look into these soap bubbles: she seemed to shudder, and she was afraid she might see something that would alarm her. In one of these she once saw a small coffin, standing before a neighboring house. At that time there was no child sick, but, shortly afterwards, the lady who lived there was confined. The child lived but a few months, and Mrs. H. saw it carried from the house in a coffin. If we wished her to recall dreams which she had forgotten, it was only necessary to make her look at a soap bubble, and her memory of them immediately returned. She often saw persons, that were about to arrive at the house, in a glass of water; but when she was invited to this sort of divination, and did it unwillingly, she was sometimes mistaken.[5]

In the nineteenth century, it was known that people in a clairvoyant state could read what was placed on the pit of their stomach, or solar plexus, as we now call it. The Seeress was able to do this also. Writings or drawings placed on the pit of her stomach produced sensations according to the nature and meaning of what was on the papers.

The next claim of hers seems bizarre. She claimed she could see people on the moon:

A magnetic wand, with an iron point, held to her right eye, and directed to any distant object, magnified it exceedingly: The smallest star appeared as large as the moon, and the moon so large, that she could distinguish the different bright spots. But she could only discern the right side of it; the left was invisible to her. She said that the dwellers on the left side of the moon were much engaged with building, and not so happy as those on the right. I told her I thought this was mere dreaming; but she denied it, and said that her sleep-waking was a state of perfect vigilance. It is much to be regretted, that these observations were made, at a time that the Seeress was unable to leave her bed, and a long contemplation of the heavenly bodies was out of her power.[6]

Was she actually seeing physical people on the moon? Since we have been to the moon and have not discovered any life or any evidence of past life there, it appears she may have been wrong. But it is interesting to note that both Swedenborg and Andrew Jackson Davis described advanced or human life on other planets. Some have suggested that they were describing not physical life, but a higher-dimensional life that inhabits the moon and the planets.

On observing an individual who had lost a limb, the Seeress still saw the limb attached to the body. It seems that she saw the aura of the person's spirit, which would always appear to be complete regardless of the physical form of the body. In Kirlian photography (which claims to be able to photograph a person's aura), if you take a photo of a leaf from which a part has been cut off, the complete leaf can be seen. This phenomenon also seems to occur with Kirlian photographs of amputated limbs: a complete aura of the limb is seen in the photographs. Also, many who have had a limb removed claim still to have a sensation in the amputated part of the body as if the limb is still there. This is called the phantom limb phenomenon, and there may be more to this than the explanation that the remaining nerve endings cause this sensitivity, as doctors claim. Could it be that this sensation is caused by the spiritual essence of the limb that was removed?

The Seeress claimed to have a visible and constant spiritual guide, who, as noted, she believed was that of her deceased grandmother. As mentioned before, she also conversed with many diverse spirits, but she did not seek out this communication, and in fact tried to avoid it. If the spirit insisted, or if she felt it was important to contact this spirit, she would enter into communication with it. She was also able to see the guarding spirit of the person she was looking at:

> She was very unwilling to converse, and never did it except when requested. . . . At such times as the faculty of ghost-seeing was active in her, she believed herself to be awake; but she was then in that peculiar state we have denominated as the inner-life. Her grandmother always appeared to her in the form she bore when alive, but in different attire: she seemed to wear a robe, with a girdle; and on her head was something like a veil, which covered the hair and fell over the ears. All female spirits, without exception, had this head-covering.[7]

It is very interesting that all female spirits had head coverings. In the Catholic Church, especially many years ago, women were required to attend mass wearing a head covering. This was a tradition that does not seem to exist anymore. Was there a spiritual reason for this that the Church was not aware of? What other religions require women to wear head coverings? Islamic religion seems to be another. I wonder what the spiritual significance of this is and how its meaning may have been lost over time.

The Seeress made a very interesting observation regarding the age that a spirit appears to be. The question arises about what happens to a child who dies. Does it always appear to be a child in its spirit body, or does its spirit age in the spiritual world?

Dr. Kerner gives an explanation: "Behind a servant girl, who lived with me, she often saw the form of a boy about twelve years old. I asked the girl if she had any relation of that age, but she said she had not. But she told me afterwards that, on thinking of my inquiry, she remembered that her brother, who had died when he was three years old, would have been just twelve."[8]

So it appears that spirits do age up to a certain point, which seems to be the ideal age for humans, about thirty. I believe time is different in the spiritual world, so we can't make any specific conclusions about this.

Andrew Jackson Davis also stated that a person who died in infancy or as a child continues to develop in the spiritual world as he would on Earth. This increase in age may just be something representative to us to signify that the spirits do mature to a perfect age.

I relate here some examples that Dr. Kerner gave of the Seeress's second sight.

On the 13th January 1827, Mrs. H. being seized with spasms at a very unusual hour, I endeavored to learn from her the cause of the accident; and, when she was in a sleep-waking state, she told me that she had seen a bier, and on it a person very dear to her—it was her brother, over whom a great danger impended; he would be shot at on the 18th of the month; and she pointed out how he should escape the danger, and described the assassin. It happened as she had foretold; but the shot missed him. Some time after she had another warning respecting her brother: several times in her magnetic sleep she saw a fox, and she became aware that, in chasing this animal, he would be in imminent danger from the charge of his gun. Her brother, being warned, examined his weapon, and found that some unfriendly hand had overcharged it; and he thus escaped the danger. She was supposed to be much *en rapport* with this brother, he having frequently magnetized her.

On the morning of the 8th of May, at seven o'clock, she bade her sister not come too near her bed, for she felt that something invisible was approaching. She had had this feeling for an hour, and was eating her breakfast, when she saw her dead child standing by the bed, and near it her living one, which was far away. The dead one looked on her steadfastly, and pointed with the finger to the living one. The latter had a pin in its hand, which it held in its mouth. The children appeared so real and actual, that she stretched out her hand to take away the pin. She cried out "In the name of God, what is this?" and then the vision disappeared. The child, which had died when it was nine months old, looked now as if it were three—which is the age it would have reached had it lived—but it was light and transparent. The aspect of both was strange—something she found it impossible to describe. This sight affected her much, and she wept. She afterwards said that, in seven days hence, her child would swallow a pin, and die of it; and that her parents, with whom the child was, must be warned of the danger. This was done; and they wrote that, on examining the child, they had found a pin in its sleeve, which they had removed.

Three successive days before the death of her father, at a time that the news of his illness had not reached her, she saw, when she was awake, a coffin standing by her bed, which was covered by a mort-cloth [shroud], on which lay a white cross. She was very much alarmed, and said she feared her father was dead, or sick. I comforted her by suggesting that some other person might be signified. She did not know how to interpret this covered coffin, as hitherto she had either seen coffins with the likeness of the person about to die lying in them, or the likeness of the person about to be sick looking into them. On the morning of the 2d of May came the news of her father's illness; on the same evening he died; whilst she in her sleep was much distressed, and intimated that she saw something grievous, which she would not tell us, in order that she might not know it when she was awake; on the next came the news of his death. Three times when awake she saw her mother-in-law looking into a coffin: seven days afterwards this lady fell ill, but she recovered. When Mrs. H. saw the image of a person lying dead in a coffin, it predicted their approaching death—if alive, a severe illness.[9]

The Seeress could clearly distinguish the internal organs of a person's body and determine if they were diseased. She distinctly saw the nerves and could anatomically describe them. Andrew Jackson Davis also had this ability to see the body transparently and could also tell which organ or organs were diseased. He said that they did not shine as brightly as the healthy ones, and he was able to diagnosis his patients this way.

The Seeress believed that certain numbers and repetitions of these numbers were necessary in the application of her prescriptions. Each person had a specific number or numbers, and the application of her remedies was based on this. For example, she considered the number seven to be her special number, and most of her remedies were to be taken on the seventh hour of the day, or for seven days. For someone else, a different number may have applied.

Regarding her specific numbers, she said, "This number lies within me like a language. Had I the number 3, I should be well much sooner."[10]

She often prescribed St.-John's-wort (*Hypericum perforatum*). She prescribed not only that it be taken internally, but also that it be used as an amulet, whereby a person would wrap the St.-John's-wort in a piece of paper or cloth and wear it around her or his neck or carry it on her or his person. Her remedies were drawn not only from the chemist's shop but also from all of nature. Some were very exotic, like her prescription of an ointment made from the nipples of a horse for strengthening the spine. Even faith and prayer were sometimes part of her prescriptions: "Her prescriptions were often in accordance with the homoeopathic system: ordering those things, in small quantities, which, in larger, would have produced the disease to be cured. Sometimes her prescriptions were purely magical. Thus, at one time she desired me, every morning and evening, at seven, to say the Lord's Prayer, provided I could do it with entire faith; and that, on repeating the words, 'Deliver us from evil,' I should lay my hand on her forehead, etc."[11]

She seldom used amulets for herself but did prescribe them more frequently for others. These amulets were sometimes composed of some vegetable substance but most often were paper with her inner writing on it. I wonder if she ever thought these remedies could be used by others after she died. It may seem strange that writing on a piece of paper could bring a cure.

Regarding this, Dr. Kerner writes:

And why should there not be a language like that the Seeress describes, which expresses, by its words and characters, the powers and gradations of physical nature; so that, by hearing or reading the words, the existing properties of the thing are immediately presented to the mind? A representative, or pictorial language, must necessarily express an entire system, in a few words; and there may thus be magical words, which comprise both the spirit and the power of holiness; and an amulet may be only a holy cipher, or property in nature, emitting the name and virtue of the true faith.[12]

The application of the amulets she prescribed was also different for each person. Sometimes she specified that they were to be "laid on the person's back or the pit of the stomach."

The idea that faith is required for healing is not a new one. She said "that to exercise magical powers, the most entire faith in the invisible world was requisite. It is a faculty of the soul, which is sustained by the spirit. There is another sort of magic—of which I shall not speak— which is not sustained by the spirit."[13]

What is this magic not sustained by the spirit? She said, "This magic is of an evil nature, and is practiced by those who have subjected themselves to evil spirits."[14]

Dr. Kerner claimed that many received favorable results from the use of her amulets and were cured by them. He says, "At all events, the results were in favor of the efficacy of the amulets. Let those who doubt, go to the spot and inquire; the witnesses are named, and still to be found."[15]

When a person with a disease approached her, she immediately became conscious of his disease and also felt his actual sensations before the person could describe them to her. She also was aware of the mental condition of each person who visited her. She said that she was aware of a person's physical condition with her body and his mental condition with her soul.

Eschenmayer validates this claim by saying that not only he himself but also numerous other witnesses could testify to this fact: "For she accurately divined my whole bodily condition, as well as that of a friend—and this, by only the contact of the hand."[16]

10

INNER LANGUAGE AND NUMBERS

What do we know about this inner language that the Seeress claimed was the language of the spirits? Is this the Primal Language that we have been talking about? Let's look more closely at her descriptions of it.[1]

As we know, the Seeress made it clear that disembodied spirits have no real need of a written and spoken language, since they read each other's thoughts. A possible reason a written and spoken language may exist in the spirit world is that it would be a mode of communication between spirits and humans. The Seeress was not only able to write with this language but could also speak it. She said it was the original language of humankind and the one that Jacob of the Bible spoke. This is further confirmation that this may be the Primal Language that the mystics of all ages have been searching for. Is it possible that this poor peasant woman was one of the chosen recipients of this language? Many who had witnessed her speaking and writing this language believed it was an actual language. She was quite consistent with its usage, and those who often heard her speak it gained some familiarity with its meanings. Does this Primal Language have to be imparted to us by an angel or another human being who knows it, or do we have the ability within ourselves to develop it?

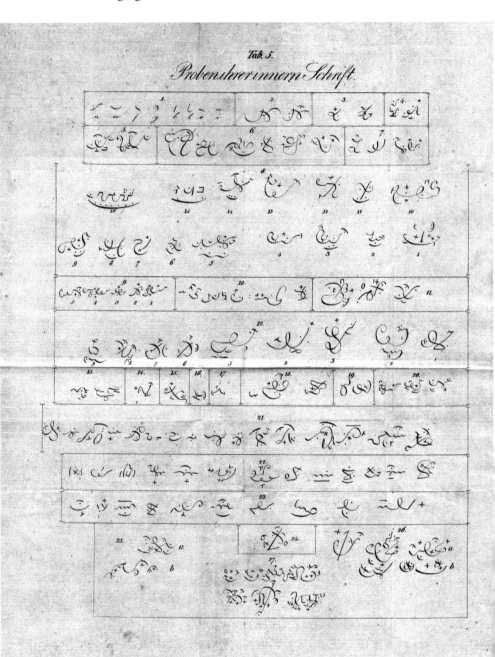

Fig. 10.1. Examples of the inner-language script of the Seeress. Image from *Die Seherin von Prevorst: Eröffnungen über das innere Leben des Menschen und über das Hereinragen einer Geisterwelt in die unsere.*

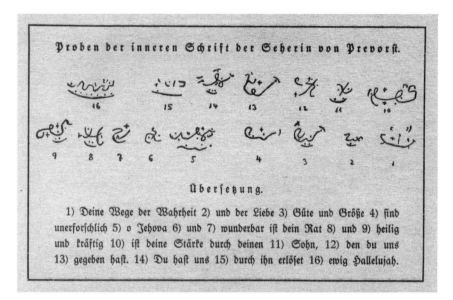

Fig. 10.2. More examples of the inner-language script of the Seeress. Image from *Die Seherin von Prevorst und die Botschaft Justinus Kerner*, by Justinus Kerner and von Felix Kretschmar.

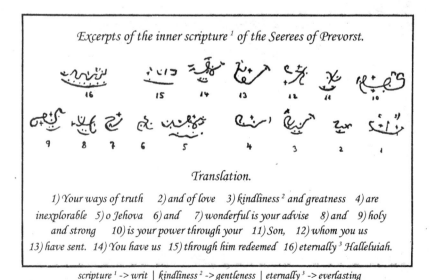

Fig. 10.3. English translation of figure 10.2 above. Translated by and courtesy of George Setian.

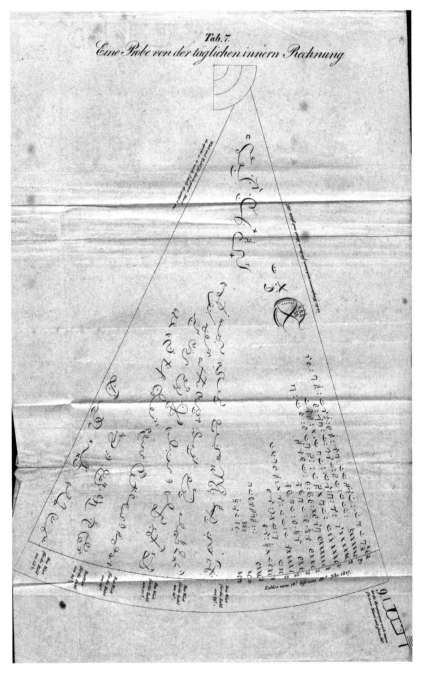

Fig. 10.4. The inner-language script of the Seeress. Image from *Die Seherin von Prevorst: Eröffnungen über das innere Leben des Menschen und über das Hereinragen einer Geisterwelt in die unsere.*

She said that this inner spiritual language was latent and undeveloped in every human being. At the time of death, when the person leaves the body, he or she will speak it instinctively. People who heard her speak it described the sound as sonorous and said that it resembled an Oriental tongue. It's unfortunate that we don't have a recording of it; the first tape recorders were invented by German engineers in the 1930s.

The Seeress said this language was connected with numbers, and therefore possessed an infinitely greater expression than any outward language. It appears to bear a resemblance to Coptic, Arabic, and Hebrew. It is interesting to note that Hebrew also does not have a number system, but each letter corresponds to a numerical value. This is true of the Greek and Akkadian languages also. Both the writing and the numbers of this inner language went from right to left, similar to Oriental writing. A well-known ancient language expert told me that the characters resemble Arabic with a flourish. He identified it as medieval angelic language and said it was the language that certain mystics used during medieval times, by which they claimed to communicate with angels.

When the Seeress was awake and not in her clairvoyant state, she had no knowledge of this language and could not speak or write it. She said that the words of this language contain the value and properties of the things they express. As an example, she said her name in the inner language was Emelachen, which she said expressed entirely her character and being. She wrote this name in her German script and not the inner language so that her friends and Kerner could pronounce it. Other examples she gave include the word Elschaddai, which she often used for God. The term signifies "self-sufficient or all-powerful." The word *bianachli* signifies "I am sighing."

Following are a few of the words of this inner language and their interpretations:

handacadi = physician
alentana = lady

chlann = glass

schmado = moon

nohin = no

nochiane = nightingale

bianna fina = many-colored flowers

moy = how

toi = what

optini poga = thou must sleep

mo li arato = I rest

Elschaddai = self-sufficient or all-powerful God

bianachli = I am sighing

She also said that everyone has two personal inner numbers. Her numbers were ten and seventeen. The first number, ten, represents the number of all humankind and the person's relationship to the physical world. The second number represents a person's inner or spiritual life. Individuals will take these numbers with them when they die so that at the time of death, they can review their entire life using this one number.

This second number also indicates or represents the duration of that individual's life. There is, in this number, a spiritual value that determines the law of one's development and the maximum length of one's life. We receive this number at birth; it reflects the maximum age we may attain, and we cannot live beyond it. The Seeress said, however, that we may die before this time if we exhaust this number. By neglecting or abusing the body, a person may shorten his or her life and not reach the allotted number. He or she may also die before the time indicated if an accident occurs. It is interesting that the Seeress said that there is a daily waste of vitality in each person, but this is also compensated for on a daily basis. After middle age, however, the body loses its energy and nutritive powers faster than can be compensated for, and the body gradually declines.

All our actions and thoughts are recorded, and according to the Seeress, "Worse than neglecting of good is the doing of evil."[2] So in our tally sheet, there is a constant moral loss or gain, depending on our actions, that are recorded forever. We will be able to read the total experience of our life when we die with this inner numbering system: "Immediately after death, that natural language, which lies in every man, is revealed to him, and he reads at once his whole life, with its acts and omissions, in its characters. The account is engraven on his heart in figures of fire."[3]

One day when she was trying to translate her own name into a figure, she suddenly burst into tears. Dr. Kerner asked her what she was upset about. She said that she had suddenly come upon a much deeper secret connected with numbers, which she had discovered by accident. She had discovered the date and hour of her death. Kerner told her he thought it impossible that anyone could calculate the time of death by her name, but she answered, "When you die, you will learn that it is possible."[4]

Besides the above explanations of these inner numbers, there appeared to her another, deeper and higher significance, the explanation of which she refused to give. So it appears there are levels of meaning with this inner language and numbers. Could one possibility be that the pronunciation of the name of an object using this inner language would affect it physically, perhaps by resonance?

We do have a very interesting and important clue about the Seeress's language and number system. It seems that it's based on a septenary numeral system, which is a base-7 system, instead of a base-10 like our number system. Our system has ten digits: 0123456789. The base-7 system uses only the following digits: 0123456. Thus, the representation of a quantity is different for each of the systems: in a base-7, the number 7 is represented by 10, since you have 1 seven and 0 ones, and the number 8 is represented by 11, because you have 1 seven and 1 one, etc.

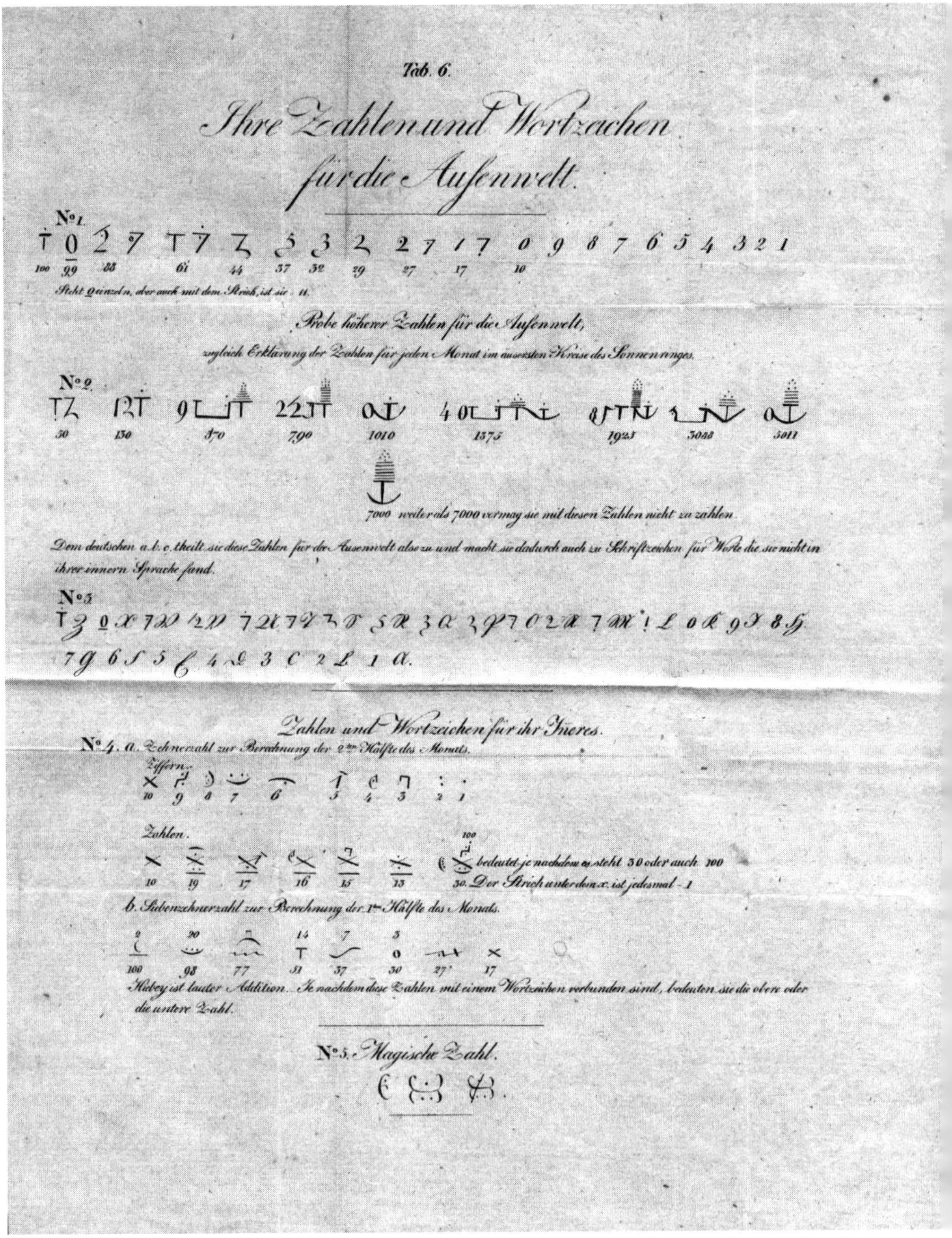

Fig. 10.5. A table of the numeric inner language of the Seeress. Image from *Die Seherin von Prevorst: Eröffnungen über das innere Leben des Menschen und über das Hereinragen einer Geisterwelt in die unsere.* (See translation on page 118.)

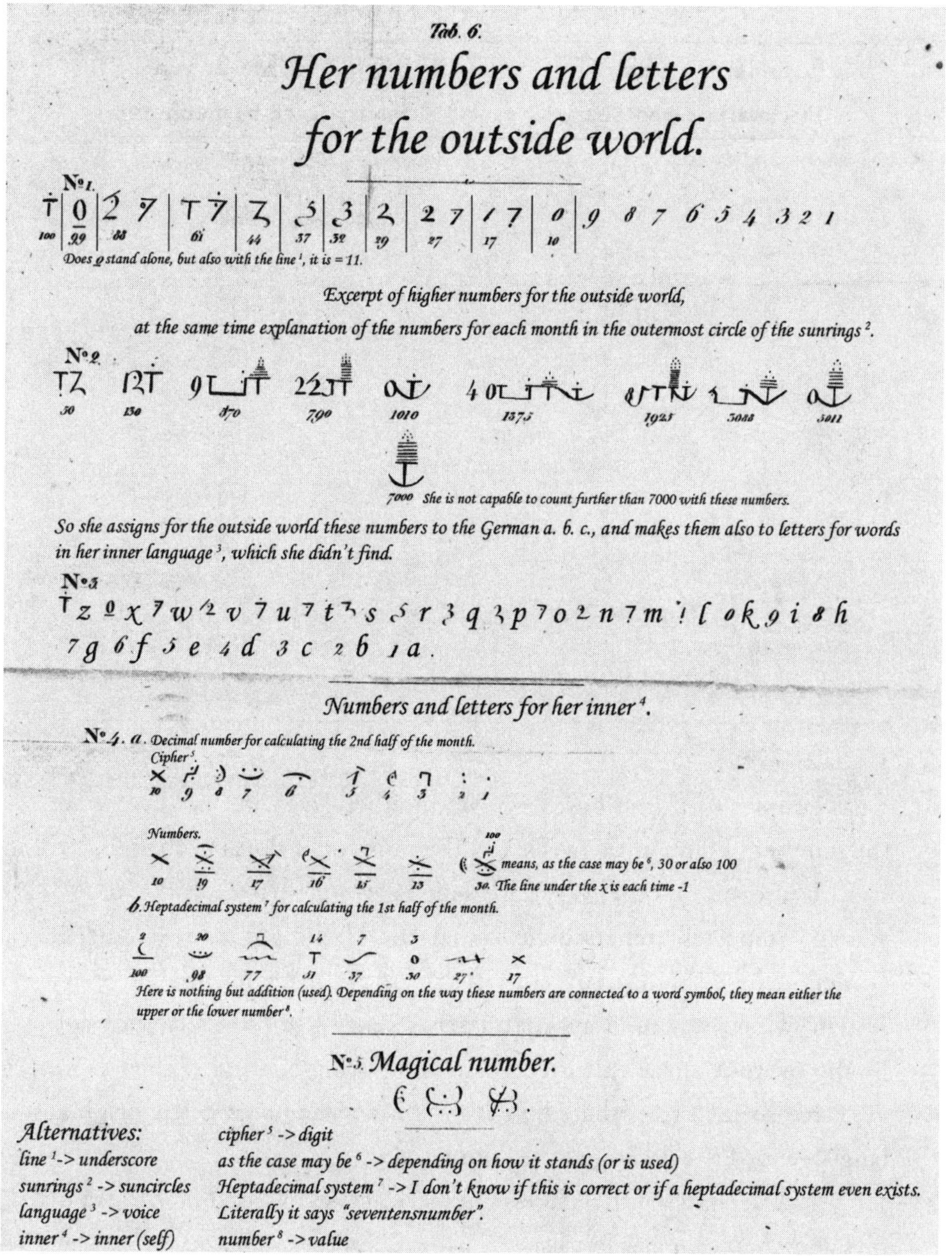

Tab. 6.

Her numbers and letters
for the outside world.

N⁰ 1.

Does 0 stand alone, but also with the line¹, it is = 11.

Excerpt of higher numbers for the outside world,
at the same time explanation of the numbers for each month in the outermost circle of the sunrings².

N⁰ 2.

7000 She is not capable to count further than 7000 with these numbers.

So she assigns for the outside world these numbers to the German a. b. c., and makes them also to letters for words in her inner language³, which she didn't find.

N⁰ 3.

Numbers and letters for her inner⁴.

N⁰ 4. *a.* Decimal number for calculating the 2nd half of the month.
Cipher⁵.

Numbers.

means, as the case may be⁶, 30 or also 100
30. The line under the x is each time -1

b. Heptadecimal system⁷ for calculating the 1st half of the month.

Here is nothing but addition (used). Depending on the way these numbers are connected to a word symbol, they mean either the upper or the lower number⁸.

N⁰ 5. Magical number.

Alternatives:

line¹ -> underscore	cipher⁵ -> digit
sunrings² -> suncircles	as the case may be⁶ -> depending on how it stands (or is used)
language³ -> voice	Heptadecimal system⁷ -> I don't know if this is correct or if a heptadecimal system even exists.
inner⁴ -> inner (self)	Literally it says "seventensnumber".
	number⁸ -> value

Fig. 10.6. English translation of figure 10.5. Translated by and courtesy of George Setian.

A COMPARISON OF BASE-NUMBER SYSTEMS

Base-10	Base-7	Base-2
Decimal	Septenary	Binary (used by computers)
0	0	0
1	1	1
2	2	10
3	3	11
4	4	100
5	5	101
6	6	110
7	10	111
8	11	1000
9	12	1001
10	13	1010
11	14	1011

Examples of things based on the number seven in our society are the number of days in the week and the number of notes in the musical scale. It also appears that very early languages were based on this base-7 system. Some researchers believe that the Uralic group of languages (which includes Hungarian and Finnish) shows evidence of a septenary system, which was used approximately twenty-five hundred years ago by the proto-Magyar culture. This is interesting because it adds more evidence to the claim that the Seeress's inner language is the original language, or Primal Language of humankind.

I have deciphered the Seeress's numerical system based on the examples and charts she has left us.

It is very difficult to explain, but the general idea is that the counting is based upon certain symbols that add value to the base number. For example, a value of 100 was assigned to a numerical system that looks like a *T* with a line or dot over it. The line means 100, and the dot reinforces it. If there are two lines, its value is 200, and there may be two dots over the two lines to reinforce that. A *T* with five lines over it and with or without the five dots would be equal to 500, and so on. Now if you take the *T* with the dot over it, which equals 100, and add a semicircle under it, its value changes to 1,000. A *T* with two lines and two dots over it with the semicircle under would equal 2,000. Now, there is some variation. A single *T* without any dot is equal to 61. A single *T* with a dot under it is equal to six, and as we said before, a *T* with a dot over it is equal to 100. It gets more complicated with certain numbers, but in general it is a well-defined number system based on seven.

The Seeress also used dots and squiggles to change the value of a number. For example, the number 2 has a value of two, but if a dot is put on its left side, it equals 20. A squiggle on the top of the 2 with the dot would equal 88. I discovered this by looking at many examples. She also said that the highest number she could represent was 7,000. This analysis is important, since it shows that her number system is a real system and not just a bunch of arbitrary numbers and values; it really makes sense.

This inner-number system, as she described it, is also used to keep track of all of our thoughts, words, and actions. These values are tallied up at the end of each day and then summed up at the end of each month. A symbol indicates this sum for each month. Nothing escapes God, and this record of all our thoughts, words, and deeds, as represented by numeric symbols, follows us all our lives and into death. It is our karma or Hall of Records.

11

THE SUN
AND LIFE SPHERES

Besides this inner language discussed in the previous chapter, the Seeress constructed diagrams that she called inner circles. She had drawn eight of them. Seven are called Sun Circles and one is called the Life Circle. She also referred to them as the Sun and Life Spheres, since they were actually three-dimensional spheres that she drew in two-dimensional projections on paper. She said they were the "prophecy of her future" and the "day-book of her past." She labeled these circles with script from her inner language and numbers. The Sun Circles, which are the outer circles in this series, are the "sphere of the spirit," and the Life Circle, which is the interior one, is the "sphere of the soul, or mental-life."[1]

I must point out that these Sun Circles were not just a theoretical construct for her but were real objects that she said encircled her and were fastened to her left side. She said that the orbits of these circles seemed to come out from the pit of her stomach, pass over the chest, and pass around close by the left side. You can picture this as a sphere of about ten inches in diameter placed in the left-front side of the body and including within it the heart and part of the stomach.

She said they lay heavy upon her and on the nerves, and were composed of what she called nerve-spirit. She could actually see and feel

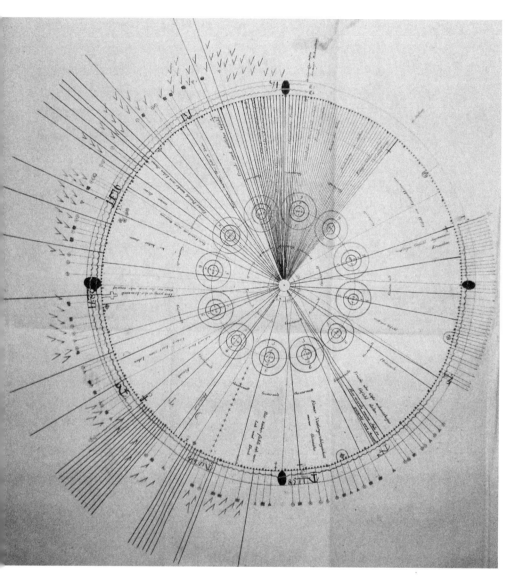

Fig. 11.1. The Sun Sphere or Circle. Image from *Die Seherin von Prevorst: Eröffnungen über das innere Leben des Menschen und über das Hereinragen einer Geisterwelt in die unsere.*

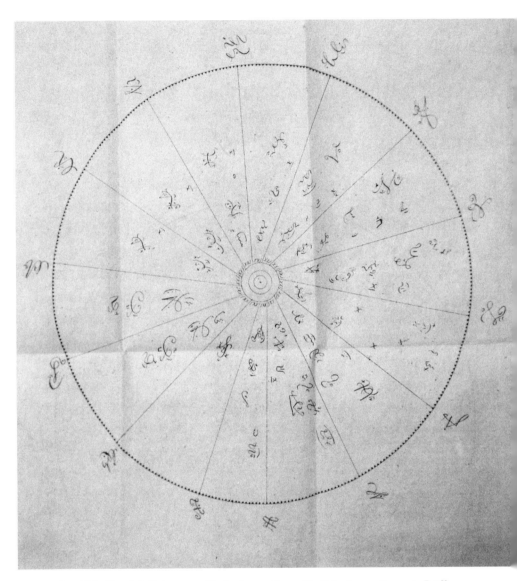

Fig. 11.2. The Life Sphere or Circle. Image from *Die Seherin von Prevorst: Eröffnungen über das innere Leben des Menschen und über das Hereinragen einer Geisterwelt in die unsere.*

these circles. These circles, she said, were always in motion, and every seven years the seven Sun Circles fell away and seven more appeared. Thus each Sun Circle represented one year.

The most remarkable thing connected with these circles is that every day the balance of a person's good and evil was summed up and expressed in a number on these circles. This balance was then carried forth into the next day, so at the end of every day, this number expresses the exact balance—for or against the individual—of all his or her thoughts, words, and deeds. As discussed in the previous chapter,

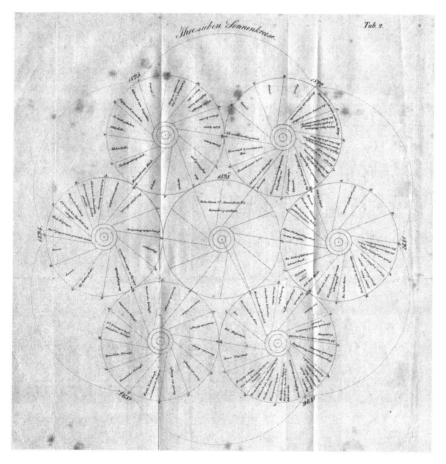

Fig. 11.3. Sun Circles for seven years of the Seeress's life (1822–1828). Image from *Die Seherin von Prevorst: Eröffnungen über das innere Leben des Menschen und über das Hereinragen einer Geisterwelt in die unsere.*

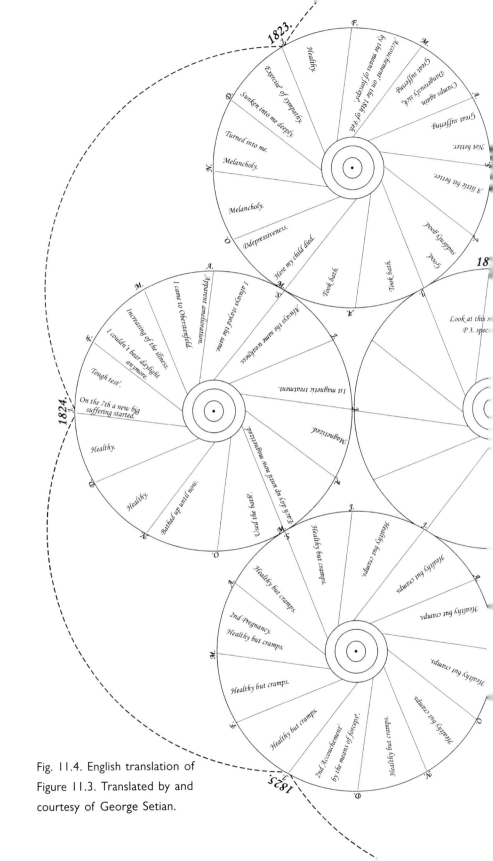

Fig. 11.4. English translation of Figure 11.3. Translated by and courtesy of George Setian.

1822.

Here I feel melancholy.
Here I wasn't in the ring yet.
Indication of my illness.
Up until now always sad.
1st attack, vehement cramp.
Applying mustard. Bloodletting
Always dying. Self-searing.
Here I came into the ring.
Day's awful. helped.
No applause.
They layed the hand on me.
Up until now no improvement.
Exercise of Sympathy.
Up until now 32 times bloodletting.
Weak.
1st pregnancy.
Here they started the homeopathic treatment.
Improvement.
I came to Oberstenfeld.
It became more and more better.
Came to Löwenstein into the health resort.
I became healthy again.
Healthy.
Healthy.
Healthy.
Healthy.

28.

venth suncircle
fly drawn.

Adverse feeling.
Homesickness.
Delight but melancholy.
Here my soul was so strengthened from the outside.
A little bit of abjection of my mind.
Up until here I feel only praise and gratitude.
Joviality.
Delight.
Praise and gratitude.
Delight to live.
Here something was going on that attacked me very much.
Up until now.
A little bit of joy. Stones.
Always Stones.
Good advancements of recovery.
Physical revival. Stones.
Delight and divine feeling.
I only lived in the spiritual vision.
Here my hearing passed off.
Adverse feeling unchanged.

1827.

More and more sick.
This continued.
Acutely affected.
Awful emesis".
Here I came back again.
Here I made a trip.
Good.
Good. Magnetic.
Better. Magnetic.
Here it was better. Came then into magnetic state.
Thereupon I first became wild and ???
Here I got a fever in the childhood and the old ill came back.
Exercise of Sympathy.
Fear of everything. Sad and afraid.
Here I first became wild and ???
Great hope for healthiness.
Magnetized.
Heavenly joy.
Divine comfort".
Struggle for health.
Desire" to die.
Fell to asleep, afore desperation.
Came to Weinsberg.
I didn't get into my most inner anymore. ???".
I was brought to Löwenstein.
Lament" only.

1826.

we thus have, at the end of our life, a number expressing the exact moral account of all of our thoughts and actions from that life. In our souls, this self-registering principle is always going on, the operation of which is independent of our control.

She stated that all events in our world have a number or numerical value associated with them, and she was always calculating events in her life and the current value of this number for her. Some events were "advances" and some were "losses," and this was reflected in the sum of this number.

The manner in which the Seeress drew these diagrams under spirit influence deserves special attention. Kerner says that she would throw off a whole drawing "in an incredibly short time, and employed in marking the more than a hundred points, into which this circle was divided, no compasses or instrument whatever. She made the whole with her hand alone, and failed not in a single point. She seemed to work as a spider works its geometric diagrams, without any visible instrument. I recommended her to use a pair of compasses to strike the circles; she tried, and made immediate blunders."[2]

She had two systems of calculation, one for the outer or physical world and one for the inner or spiritual world. So facile and innate was her knowledge of this language and this system of calculations that at any time afterward, she could detail in an instant any variation, however slight, in any copy of her writing or drawing. On a copy of her Sun Circle, brought to her by Dr. Kerner a year after she had made the original, she immediately detected the omission of a single point. She had kept no copy herself.

She said that every person carries on him or her these Sun and Life Spheres, which on paper look like circular calendars. The Life Circle, the inner sphere, is, in a sense, a mirror to the Sun Circles. "The soul is a mirror of the universe" is a well-known axiom among mystics. She explained that when her soul entered and occupied the center of her Sun Circle, she had the ability to see the past and the future and the infinite. She could also see the world in all the laws, relations, and properties that had been implanted in it through time and space. She saw all this clearly without any veil interposing. Apparently she would lose these abilities as she moved out from the center of this circle.

She said, "But in proportion as the soul is drawn from the center by the attractions of the outer world it advances into darkness and loses this all-embracing vision and knowledge of nature and its properties."[3] Thus most people do not and cannot occupy the center of their Sun Circles—only the prophet and advanced mystic is capable of this. The Seeress said that in the infancy of the human race, humankind lived more in this circle, and there was little or no veil between the physical world and the spiritual. But time and its increasing corruptions have drawn the human soul farther and farther from the center. They have drawn it into thick worldly darkness and engrossments, and the veils between the earthly and the divine have grown thicker.

It appears that there is some similarity between her system of circles and calculations and those of Pythagoras, and Plato also wrote of circles and inner mystical numbers. He wrote, "The soul is immortal and has an arithmetical beginning, as the body has a geometrical one. It is the image of a universally diffused spirit; has a self-movement, and penetrates from the center through the whole body around. It is, however, diffused through corresponding mid-spaces, and forms at the same time two circles bound to each other."[4]

One he calls the Movement of the Soul, which corresponds to the Life Circles of our Seeress, and the other he calls the Movement of the Universe and of the Comets, which corresponds to her Sun Circles. Plato says that by this means the soul is placed in connection with what is external, apprehends what exists, and subsists harmoniously due to the fact that it has within itself the elements of perfect harmony. The harmony of the world and the generation of all things originate from these numbers, and one who loses one's number (the sum of all the numbers from all the Sun Circles of a person's life) loses all community with what is good, and disorder and confusion are the person's portion.

This is similar to what the Seeress said: If a person loses this fundamental calculation or number, he or she is, with the consent of his or her own will, placed in immediate rapport with evil and its consequences. The Seeress's descriptions are very consistent with those of Plato, and yet she had never even heard of Plato or read anything that he had written. Similarities also exist between Frederika's theories and those of Pythagoras, who said that numbers are the elements of all things and of all knowledge.

That her Life and Sun Circles were realities to her is evidenced by the fact that she lay drawings of them on her heart, always in a particular manner in her clairvoyant sleep, and if they were slightly altered, she felt it at once and *readjusted them exactly as they had been laid before, without once looking at them.* Thus it seems that there was a real relationship between the two-dimensional drawings and the actual three-dimensional spheres that surrounded her. During one of her clairvoyant states, she said that several circles or spheres, which she had passed through, appeared to her. On the first of these spheres were seven stars, which she said were the dwellings of the blessed of inferior grades. The second sphere was of the moon, which was very cold and disagreeable. Those who were to be blessed dwelled on the right side of the moon, and here also lived many spirits who came out of the mid-region (the region where the spirits dwell before they move up into high spheres). In one of these circles, she said, she saw her protecting spirit, and in another the souls of animals. What specific spheres she was referring to is unclear.

She said that when she entered the highest state of clairvoyance, her spirit left the Life Sphere and entered the center of the Sun Sphere. When this happened, all things became visible and known to her, and she was freed from the veil or screen that otherwise concealed them. At this point she had attained the highest level of spiritual awareness possible, replete with all the psychic and clairvoyant abilities that we have previously discussed.

Apparently, the higher spiritual dimensions are open to a person in this sphere.[5] What humans used to know intuitively today must be learned. The Seeress claimed that when she attained this elevated state, she saw the whole world penetrated with light, and she saw the human being as the mirror of a divine radiance. She perceived the soul as the mirror of everything that exists. In this mirror all objects would be reflected, were they not hidden by the thick mist of earthly vapors: "The inner-sense in man is the burning light, the spirit, which, however, cannot always shine through the thick husk of the body, but, like the internal fires of the earth, can only break through at certain points; that is, only in certain men—not in the whole race. The day will come, when the whole earth will be lighted by its internal fires; so will man cast off his thick husk, and be dissolved in the universal light."[6]

This describes the future spiritual enlightenment of all humankind. Is this what is referred to as the Golden Age, the Age of Aquarius, and/or the New Millennium? An interesting point she makes is that animals such as dogs and horses are less isolated from the spiritual world than are human beings, and they are more sensitive to the presence of spirits. This can be said of saints, poets, and prophets also. Old age and childhood seem to make a person more sensitive as well.

Regarding the seven sun spheres, and as noted previously, the Seeress said that "every seven years these solar orbits fell off [me], and their entire contents could be expressed in a cipher, or a point, in which all the hours, minutes, and seconds of the seven years should be contained." It's interesting that the method by which she would be magnetized or mesmerized depended on the direction of the orbits of these circles for that current month—apparently the orbits of the circles could and did change.

Let's now look at the most detailed description she has left us regarding her Sun Sphere. The most *outer solid circle* was the boundary between the physical and the spiritual world. Outside this circumference was the physical world and inside was the spiritual world. In the physical world, she felt the spirits of all individuals known to her, although not necessarily by name, and without being able to see their bodies. As an example, at one particular point she felt Dr. Kerner as a blue flame. He was perpetually moving and accompanied by his wife a little farther off.

Given that the outer ring of the circle was the demarcation line between the physical world and the spiritual world, when the person moved inside this circle, it represented the withdrawal of his spirit from the physical world toward the spiritual world. It was a movement toward the center.

Inside this outer solid circle was a *partial wavy line* that is colored blue in the original lithograph. It lies between the two outermost peripheral solid circles. This wavy circle signified the magnetic aura of the Seeress, which was actually a magnetic wall isolating her from the outer world. It does not go the whole way around. She did not explain why and said that this magnetic aura could be produced by mesmerism.

The *second complete ring* was divided into 365 days (dots) and twelve months (segments), and from these issue the lines (radii) toward the center of the circle. From this circle, the Seeress began to develop clairvoyance. All the events of her inner life for that year would be stored in the different compartments (months) into which the radii divide this ring. At the end of each month, a number is elaborated that represents the sum of the events for that year. From month to month it became larger, till it attained a maximum value, which had its total value in the number that was specific to the Seeress.

Next, the *large space* between this second ring and the next or third solid ring represented her spirit world, where she had her encounters with spirit beings invisible to us. They came to her out of this midregion, as she calls it, "in order that, through prayer, they might regain their true relation to Christ and salvation through him."

Next, the *third solid ring* was bordered by twelve bright spheres, one in each compartment for each of the twelve months. It is here that we first have the highest level of clairvoyance and clear-seeing. Each sphere contains numbers that are variable in each individual. It is also here that the clairvoyant now has the ability to diagnose, prescribe, and perhaps predict the immediate future.

Finally, the *last three small circles around the center* were set with little stars. The Seeress said, "These stars signify nothing but stars."[7]

In the *direct center of the circle* she placed the Sun of Grace, or God, and the abode of the blessed. "No mortal eye can gaze into it. We can know no more than is revealed by the glance which flashes for a moment in the spiritual eye and even that must be instantly turned away, or be stricken blind."[8]

From these disclosures, it would appear that when the spirit of a clairvoyant goes forth into the center of this circle, all things within our solar system are unveiled to it. As the Seeress said: "In this sphere I could go backwards and forwards [in time] and see the past and the future."[9]

She was not always at the center, but occupied many different places in this circle depending on what day it was and her condition at the time. It also appeared that this circle was like a timekeeper. Regularly, at noon and midnight, the Seeress would be pushed half a point forward, moving one point in twenty-four hours. The day seemed to impel or shove her forward. Thus this circle was like a calendar in which she was embedded and driven forward through time.

Gotthilf Heinrich von Schubert, the well-known German spiritualist, who had observed the Seeress and acknowledged her abilities, gave an interesting view of the spiritual world and her circles:

To the clairvoyant, the inner world is laid open. No longer does he strive from outside to penetrate into her interior nature, but he rather glances from her center outwards. The world of nature, as seen from within, changes itself thus into a spiritual one; for, having stepped behind the veil, the spectator beholds immediately all the powers and activities of nature. Thus a new spirit-world is thrown open to the sense of sight, and it lies before it in the same clearness as the outer world in the waking state. The circles which the Seeress has circumscribed speak of a higher spiritual world. In the center of this circle, much brighter than the sun, she saw an

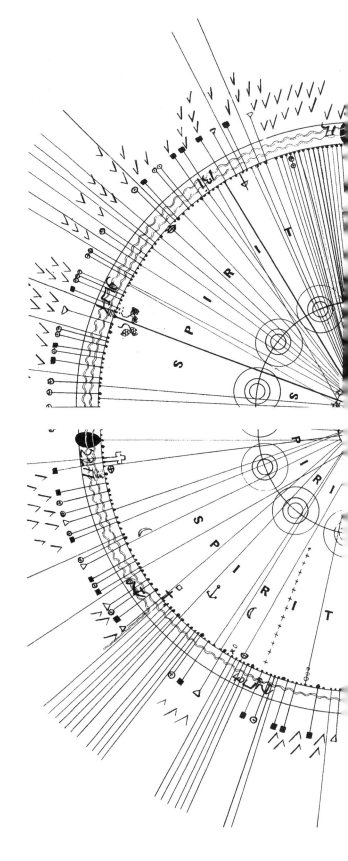

Fig. 11.5. Sun Circle, top left. Image from *The Seeress of Prevorst: Being Revelations Concerning the Inner-Life of Man, and the Inter-Diffusion of a World of Spirits in the One We Inhabit,* by Justinus Kerner, translated by Catherine Crowe.

Fig. 11.7. Sun Circle, bottom left. Image from *The Seeress of Prevorst: Being Revelations Concerning the Inner-Life of Man, and the Inter-Diffusion of a World of Spirits in the One We Inhabit,* by Justinus Kerner, translated by Catherine Crowe.

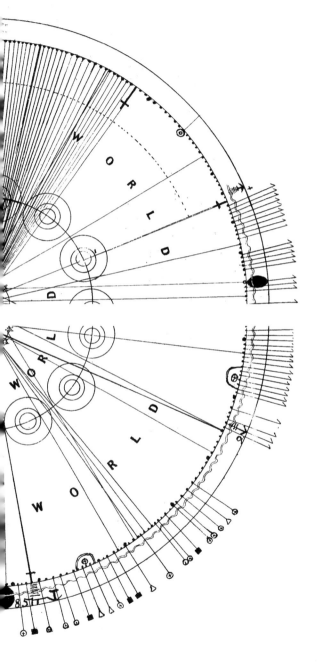

WORLD

WORLD

Fig. 11.6. Sun Circle, top right. Image from *The Seeress of Prevorst: Being Revelations Concerning the Inner-Life of Man, and the Inter-Diffusion of a World of Spirits in the One We Inhabit*, by Justinus Kerner, translated by Catherine Crowe.

Fig. 11.8. Sun Circle, bottom right. Image from *The Seeress of Prevorst: Being Revelations Concerning the Inner-Life of Man, and the Inter-Diffusion of a World of Spirits in the One We Inhabit*, by Justinus Kerner, translated by Catherine Crowe.

abyss not to be looked through, which she calls the Sun of Grace, and from which it seemed to her that all things that live precede as sparks. From there also sprung the numbers of her existence by which she conducted her calculations. This looking into the inner spiritual circle is that of the saints only, and to them alone has it been permitted to declare what they have seen. All is now sacred which before was profane.[10]

Why have we lost this ability to see the spiritual world? Dr. Kerner explains:

By the fall, the spirit has lost its integrity, and is prismatically broken; it is colored and troubled like a ray of light that has passed through a prism. The cloud of the life of appearance intercepts its view—the ideas of the true, and the beautiful, and the good, no longer exhibit themselves to it objectively, as they exist in the universal scheme. As Plato says, it has lost its wings, and, with the soul, is absorbed in the body and the world; and all that remains to it is a striving to regain those wings.[11]

The Scriptures say that man came pure from the hands of God, though he has since fallen from his purity; but that he may recover it through mediation and redemption. The cause of the fall was sin, which has not only drawn the spirit from its center, but out of its sphere; so that the worship of the one true God is split into a thousand fragments of the physical word, and a thousand idols of the human world. Truth and sin are two ever-receding poles; and we can only approach the one as we retreat from the other. There are many kinds of philosophy, but there is only one that is true; and therefore, for two thousand years the fate of all its systems have been an invariable cycle—a mere labor of Sisyphus; for no sooner have they reached their culminating points, then down they fall again.[12]

As we compare the Sun and the Life Circles, we immediately notice that they are divided into different numbers of sectors. The Life Circle contains 13¾ segments, whereas the Sun Circle contains twelve segments. Frederika called the Life Sphere "the seat of the soul," which is the sum of all the intellectual and moral faculties. She used the word *spirit* to indicate pure reason, the conscience, and the intuitive sense of the good, true, and beautiful.

She didn't leave us much information about the Life Circle, but we know it is smaller than the Sun Circles, and it is the most inner spiritual circle. The Life Circle is responsible for the sensation that we belong to the spiritual world; around it are the seven Sun Circles. She was able to describe the Sun Circles with words, but she could describe the Life Circle only with symbols that have a numeric value.

She briefly discussed the three small circles that are in the center of the Life Sphere. Inside the first circle the spirit remains in a pure and uncontaminated state. If it leaves this sphere and crosses into the second one, it becomes contaminated with worldly values and starts to lose track of the spiritual. It still has the ability to come back into the first circle on its own, and this region is still good for the person and his spirit. If the spirit leaves the second circle and crosses into the third, it moves farther away from the spiritual. The spirit has not become bad yet, but as it moves farther and farther from the first to the third circle, its uncleanness increases. Thus these three circles represent the soul straying away from the spiritual and moving toward the physical or gross world. It is obviously best for the soul to be in the center of these circles.

I hope the reader will take some time to study the Sun and Life Circles. It is my goal to bring this information to others who may discover something new about them. Each Sun and Life Circle has been divided into four sections to magnify the script and thus make it more legible.

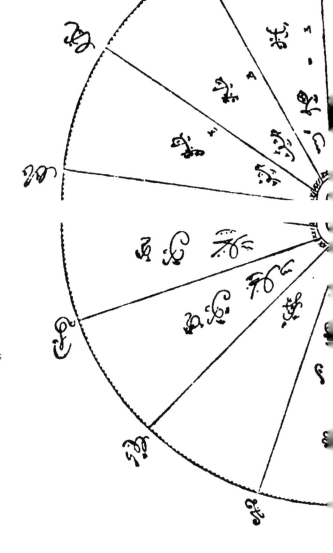

Fig. 11.9. Life Circle, top left. Image from *The Seeress of Prevorst: Being Revelations Concerning the Inner-Life of Man, and the Inter-Diffusion of a World of Spirits in the One We Inhabit*, by Justinus Kerner, translated by Catherine Crowe.

Fig. 11.11. Life Circle, bottom left. Image from *The Seeress of Prevorst: Being Revelations Concerning the Inner-Life of Man, and the Inter-Diffusion of a World of Spirits in the One We Inhabit*, by Justinus Kerner, translated by Catherine Crowe.

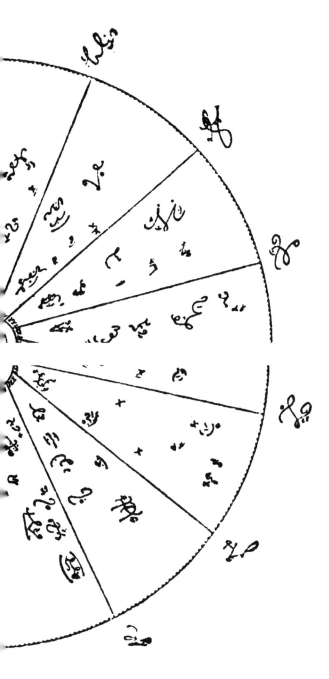

Fig. 11.10. Life Circle, top right. Image from *The Seeress of Prevorst: Being Revelations Concerning the Inner-Life of Man, and the Inter-Diffusion of a World of Spirits in the One We Inhabit,* by Justinus Kerner, translated by Catherine Crowe.

Fig. 11.12. Life Circle, bottom right. Image from *The Seeress of Prevorst: Being Revelations Concerning the Inner-Life of Man, and the Inter-Diffusion of a World of Spirits in the One We Inhabit,* by Justinus Kerner, translated by Catherine Crowe.

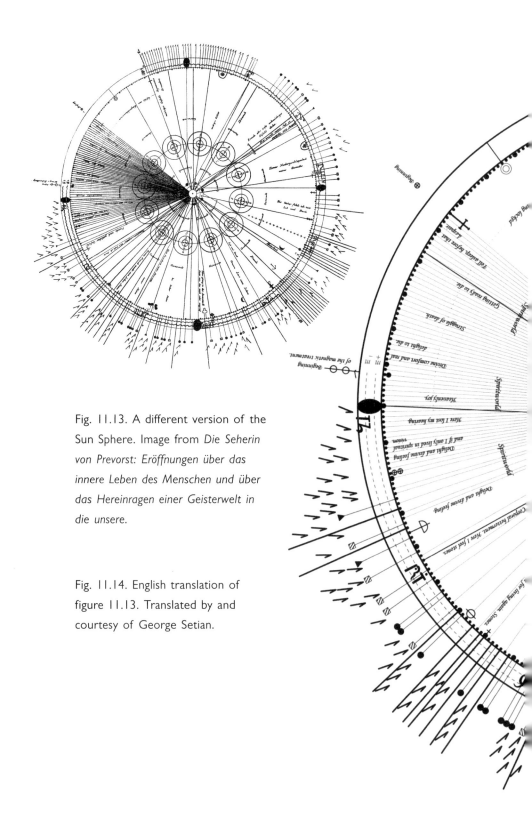

Fig. 11.13. A different version of the Sun Sphere. Image from *Die Seherin von Prevorst: Eröffnungen über das innere Leben des Menschen und über das Hereinragen einer Geisterwelt in die unsere.*

Fig. 11.14. English translation of figure 11.13. Translated by and courtesy of George Setian.

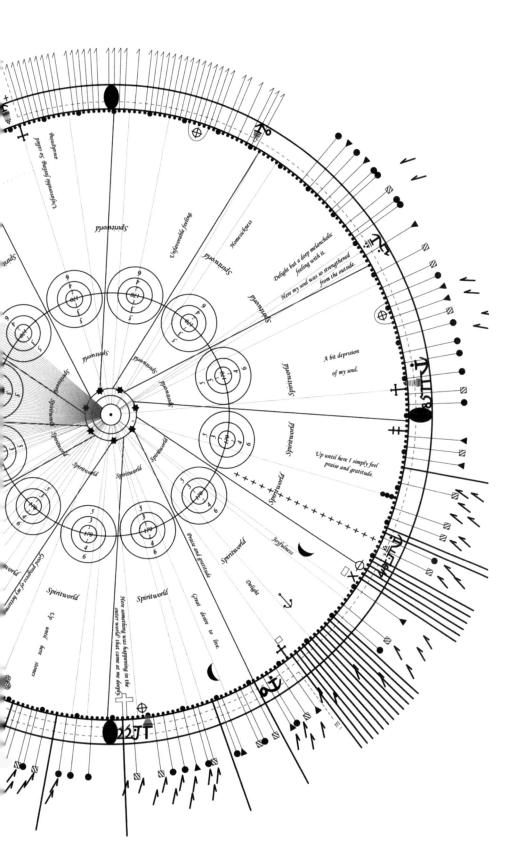

Spiritworld

Unfavorable feeling. So called awakening.

Unfavorable feeling.

Homesickness

Delight but a deep melancholic feeling with it.

Here my soul was so strengthened from the outside.

A bit deprssion of my soul.

Up until here I simply feel praise and gratitude.

Spiritworld

Spiritworld

Spiritworld

Spiritworld

Spiritworld

Spiritworld

Spiritworld

Spiritworld

Joyfulness

Praise and gratitude

Delight

Great desire to live.

Up until here states

Good prospect of my better

Here something was happening in the outer world that came at me deeply.

22JT

12
Magic and Magical Scripts

What are we really referring to when we talk about this inner or spiritual language of the Seeress? Is it similar to or the same as what we call magical language? Almost all magic, from its early beginnings in Mesopotamia and Egypt to the present time, used a magical script to invoke the spirits, angels, or gods. In fact, this is what the Primal Language tradition was based on. The same script is also contained in the Kabbalah, the ancient Jewish and later Christian mystic's handbook for contacting and controlling spirits. The practical Kabbalah uses mystical symbols, diagrams, and magical scripts to contact and control spiritual entities, whether they are angels, elementals, spirits, or archangels.

What is magic? A definition that I have developed is that magic is the carrying out of a ritual using symbols, script, and/or vocal intonations (chants) to evoke and manipulate angels or spirits to do something for you. The request could be for something physical or spiritual. If magic is used for personal and spiritual growth, it is white or good magic. White magic is used solely for spiritual motives—that is, spiritual knowledge, development, and awareness. This is also known as the Great Work. The best use of magic is for spiritual self-knowledge and self-discovery.

If it is used for selfish or evil purposes, it is considered black magic.

There are shades in between these two categories. For example, if you use magic to try to help someone who is sick, you are using magic for a good purpose, but it is not pure white magic since there is still some selfishness involved.

One of the best-known magicians of the twentieth century was Israel Regardie. He said magic is a spiritual quest that offers something eternal and enduring.[1] To many people, magic is a way to achieve spiritual growth, and the use of it is an attempt to fulfill the injunction Know thyself. When we stray from this type of magic, we enter the realm of black magic or witchcraft. It's the same with almost every religion and belief; there is the right-hand path and the left-hand path. I think this is the case with almost everything. Someone in one of my classes once asked me if computers were evil. I answered no; they can be used for good or evil—it's up to the person using them. God has given us many wonderful things, and whether we use them for good or for ill is up to us. Maybe that is a fair way to measure the level of spiritual advancement of a society.

H. P. Blavatsky said that magic is as old as humankind itself, and it is impossible to name a time or epoch when it didn't exist. It's possible that magic may have originated in the following manner: When primitive humans felt threatened by either real or imaginary ghosts or evil beings, they developed rituals and what we call magical practices as weapons to protect them from these supernatural beings. Thus, we have the primitive beginnings of magic. These rituals may have taken the form of hand gestures, vocal sounds or yelling, dancing, or throwing objects. It would be what the imagination inspired primitive humans to invent to combat the threatening appearance of these supernatural beings. To early humans, spirits lurked everywhere, especially at night.

There were good spirits and bad spirits. Human beings themselves could be in control of magic powers and use them for good or evil against others; thus was protection needed. Everyone has heard of the evil eye, whereby a person puts a curse on another person.

The Sumerian civilization is one of the earliest-known human civilizations. It developed in the Tigris-Euphrates Valley about 3000 BCE. Other early civilizations include the Acadians, the Babylonians, and the Assyrians. The language they used was cuneiform, which was written on clay tablets. Archaeologists have uncovered libraries of these tablets, which contained magical texts. Some were incantations to their gods and also were used to conjure up spirits. They included specific words to recite, songs to sing, ritual movements of the body, and the use of incense. The goal of those invoking the magic was to attract the spirits or gods to help them or protect them from something specific. Everyone accepted and used this practice—it was considered to be a normal part of society. Whether people could see the spirit didn't matter; they believed that these forces existed and could physically affect them.

As civilizations came and went, magic continued to be part and parcel of these cultures. Many people don't realize that the Bible contains many examples of magic, which the Hebrews used. If you ask a member of the clergy about magic, he or she would probably tell you that the Jews and now the Christians oppose the use of magic, as it is tampering with and usurping God's powers and authority. But there are many examples of the use of magic being condoned in the Bible. Consider the miracles of Moses, the divination of Joseph, and many others in stories from the Hebrew Scriptures.

One important point is that many scholars and scientists today do not believe in the reality of magic or a spiritual world. They believe all these experiences are imaginary and occurring inside a person. They do not believe in ghosts or spirits or even angels affecting humans in any way. How many times have you asked yourself whether magic is real?

As a child, perhaps you wondered if there was a real magical language, and if you knew certain words of it you could do supernatural things. We all grew up watching a magician say something like "Abracadabra" and then something astounding would happen, like birds flying out of a hat. Maybe as children we believed that this was real magic, and learned only later it was a trick. What about the story in the *Arabian Nights* where the words "Open sesame" would open the door to a cave where treasure was buried? We can go on and on with stories and myths that are common knowledge, but is there any truth to these stories and legends? Are they based on real factual history, now forgotten or lost, about a real magical language whose words can produce miracles just by being spoken?

Is this so far-fetched? Even today, many of our movies are based on a magical theme. In the popular *Lord of the Rings* saga, the group or fellowship comes to a place with a magic door. This door will open only if they know the password, and it must be in the Elvin language. Just look at the sensation of the Harry Potter books and movies. These stories all involve the use of magical words that have power.

Today, there appears to be a revival of and great interest in the mystical and magical Kabbalah. In fact, many well-known celebrities have been studying it, including Britney Spears and Madonna. In 2004, Madonna traveled to the Holy Land to visit historic Kabbalah sites. Madonna also sings Kabbalah praises on one of her albums, entitled *Ray of Light,* which was issued in 1998. During some of her performances, texts from the Hebrew Kabbalah, *The 72 Names of God,* flash in the background. The names of God are words of power. In 2003, she introduced Spears to the Kabbalah. Spears currently attends a church that studies and practices its use. The type of Kabbalah known as "practical Kabbalah" is basically magic.

What if I told you that millions of average people every week participate in a ritual that resembles magic rites and uses magical words? When Catholics attend Mass, they witness the priest doing something that involves mystical words. At a certain time during the Mass, the Consecration, the priest says specific words over ordinary bread and wine and claims that they have been changed into the body and blood of Jesus Christ. The Catholic Church believes that this change, which it calls transubstantiation, really occurs and is not just symbolism, as many Protestant faiths believe. Catholics also claim that although we still see only the bread and the wine, it has really been changed to the body and blood of Jesus even though we are not able to perceive it on a physical level.

It is important to note that the priest must say these specific words or this will not occur. In a magic ritual, specific words must also be used. Another thing to realize is that not just anyone can do this—one must be an ordained Catholic priest. To become an ordained priest, in a special ceremony, a bishop who has specific powers says certain words over the priest to confer this power to him. Whatever you want to call this, millions of people every week are witnessing the use of words of supernatural power. I want to be clear in that I personally do not believe that this is pure imagination and superstition, but that there is a real mystical effect in this consecration of the host. Many non–Roman Catholic mystics, like C. W. Leadbeater, have also attested to something supernatural occurring during the consecration that is beyond logical understanding. I have experienced this supernatural phenomenon as well. The Egyptians and Babylonians also appeared to worship an emblem that looked like a communion host used in exposition of the blessed sacrament and attributed supernatural meaning to this.

What about the use of prayer? Many times we say prayers to ask God or our guardian angels for something. Even though our prayers may be for the good of humanity, isn't this still magic? *Magic* is defined as carrying out a ritual to manipulate the angels or spirits to do something for you or someone else. Isn't this what certain forms of prayers try to accomplish? There are categories of prayer that do not fall into the definition of magic—for example adoration, contrition, and thanksgiving. Supplication is the type of prayer considered to be magic, since we are asking God or the angels to do something for us.

Perhaps magic is not as foreign to our everyday life as we think it is. Since the use of magic necessitates using words of power, could this be the remnant of the angelic language we are searching for?

I am not advocating magic or spiritualism for the average person, since there are inherent dangers and risks involved. You are opening doors to worlds and realities that you may not be able to close, something like opening Pandora's box, perhaps. Most well-known magicians, like Israel Regardie, always advised that practitioners undergo years of psychological counseling to ensure that they were stable and would be able to handle the performing of magic. Also, given that the Seeress said that the lower and more ignorant spirits are very willing to communicate with us, we must exercise caution, as we may be getting advice from false spirits. Disastrous things could happen if we think we are getting a message from God or an angel and it is actually from a lying and deceitful spirit with its own agenda.

Was the Seeress's use of her inner language magic? She did predict events and diagnose and prescribe treatments for others, but did she use her inner language to try to change the future or to ask for things? I don't believe she used her language in any selfish way, only to help others. She obviously knew its power, but she was also very spiritual in the sense that she believed in God and God's providence, and she believed in Jesus Christ. The Seeress apparently attributed special power and benefits from using the name of Jesus; we find that she used it in many of her remedies and protections. Mystics throughout the ages have also attributed power and protection to the name of Jesus. As we have seen, many well-known figures in the Bible, including Moses and Joseph, have used this power for good and to fulfill God's will. We may think that using magic impinges upon God's domain, but maybe it's a force God gives us to use for good or for evil, and it can be used to help carry out God's will and plans for humanity.

What is the origin of magical symbols and script? We need to go back to the Renaissance to further explore this. Dr. John Dee is considered to be one of the most important magicians or magi who ever lived.[2] He was born in London in 1527 and died in 1609. He was an accomplished scholar and author and is noted for advancing mathematics. In fact, he wrote the preface for the first English edition of Euclid's *Elements* and gave many illuminating lectures on mathematics. He was a real pioneer in this field. He was also an astronomer, geographer, alchemist, and adviser to Queen Elizabeth I. An expert navigator, he trained many famous English explorers. He proposed the expansion of the British Empire and was, in fact, the first to coin that term. His passion was for the occult, and he believed that science and the occult went hand in hand, and were not separate disciplines.

As a boy, Dee was instructed in grammar and Latin. At the age of nine or ten he was sent to the Chantry School at Chelmsford. At fifteen he left Chelmsford to enter St. John's College at Cambridge, from which he graduated in 1546 with a bachelor's degree. At the close of the same year, he was selected as one of the original Fellows at Trinity College and also appointed "under-reader" in Greek. He turned to other studies and became a skillful astronomer, taking "thousands of observations (very many to the hour and minute) of the heavenly influences and operations actual in this elementall portion of the world,"[3] which he later published as ephemerides.

In May 1547, Dee made his first journey abroad, to confer with learned men of the Dutch universities about the science of mathematics, to which he had already begun to devote his serious attention. He

Fig. 12.1. Sixteenth-century portrait of Dr. John Dee in the Ashmolean Museum, Oxford University.

spent several months in the Low Countries, forming close friendships with Gerard Mercator, Gemma Frisius, Joannes Caspar Myricaeus, the Orientalist Antonius Gogava, and other philosophers of worldwide fame. When he returned to Cambridge, he brought with him two great globes of Mercator's making, and an astronomer's armillary ring and staff of brass, "such as Frisius had newly devised and was in the habit of using."[4] Dee returned to Cambridge in 1548 to study for his master's degree, and soon thereafter he went abroad again. In 1548 he entered the University of Louvain. At Louvain, Dee continued his studies for two years, and soon acquired a reputation for learning quite beyond his years. It has been presumed that he graduated from there as a doctor (which would account for the title by which he was known).

He returned to England in 1551, and in 1553 produced *The Cause of Floods and Ebbs* and *The Philosophical and Political Occasions and Names of the Heavenly Asterismes*. When Mary Tudor succeeded her young brother in 1553, Dee was invited to calculate the new queen's natal chart. He soon began a correspondence with Princess Elizabeth, who was then living at Woodstock, and he cast her horoscope also. In 1558, when Princess Elizabeth became Queen Elizabeth, she asked Dee, an expert astrologer, to calculate the best date for her coronation. Dee also became a loyal and trusted adviser to her.[5]

Dee had a grand idea to create a State National Library of books and manuscripts, with copies of foreign treasures wherever they might be. On January 15, 1556, he presented to Queen Mary "a Supplication for the recovery and preservation of ancient writers and monuments." Nothing came of Dee's proposal, so he became all the more industrious in collecting a library of his own, which soon consisted of more than four thousand volumes. These books were always at his disposal, and at the disposal of the many friends who often came to see him.

He moved in with his mother in a house belonging to her at Mortlake, on the Thames. It was a rambling old place, standing west of the church between it and the river. Dee added to it by degrees, purchasing small tenements adjoining, so that eventually it contained libraries, laboratories for his experiments, and rooms for a busy hive of workers and servants. He published his first alchemical or metaphysical work in 1564, entitled *Monas Hieroglyphica*. In 1570 he was asked to write the preface to the first English edition of Euclid's *Elements,* the most important mathematical work at that time.[6]

In 1575, at the age of forty-eight, Dee married and on July 13, 1579, Dee's eldest son, Arthur, was born. He eventually had seven more children. Sometime in the 1580s, he became increasingly interested in the occult. He hired several individuals who he believed had the gift of contacting angels by crystal gazing. He was not really satisfied with them until he happened to meet a most gifted crystal gazer (called a scryer), whose name was Edward Kelly. Together they produced volumes of transcripts of contact with angels.[7] The angels taught them the angelic language, sometimes called the Enochian Language, since it was the language that Enoch of the Bible knew and that was also taught by the angels. Dee's diaries containing his angelic communications were published many years after his death in 1659; we are very lucky to have this important documentation.

What's so fascinating is that the angels taught him the actual angelic language, the specific names of the angels, and the angelic calls or evocations. Angel calls are the specific words one would say to call or evoke a specific angel to one's presence. This is significant because almost all modern magical societies, from the nineteenth century to the present, including the Golden Dawn and Aleister Crowley's Ordo Templi Orientis (OTO),* are based on the information in Dee's diaries. It seemed that Dee had all the theories and information, but these societies put them together in a practical format. Dee, in my opinion, is the father of modern magic.

I was hoping that in comparing the angelic language of Dr. Dee

---

*The Golden Dawn, a magical order founded in 1888, was known as the Esoteric Order of the Golden Dawn. Its purpose was to preserve the Western esoteric traditions. Ordo Templi Orientis was a magical order founded by Aleister Crowley at the beginning of the twentieth century.

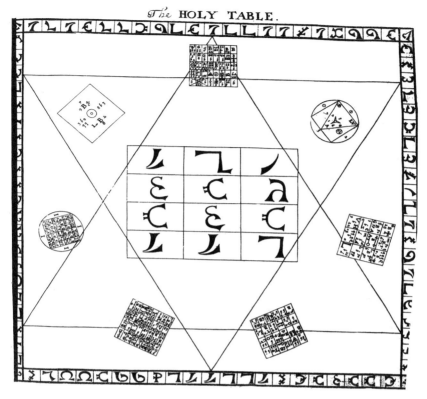

Fig. 12.2. Dee's Angelic Language. Image from *A True and Faithful Relation of What Passed for Many Years Between Dr. John Dee and Some Spirits.*

and that of the Seeress of Prevorst, I would find strong similarities. If we look at the alphabet of the angelic or Enochian language that Dee produced, there is not any obvious similarity. If you study them, however, some similarities can be found here and there. The Seeress's inner-language looks more primitive and more basic than Dee's angelic language. I believe both these languages came from the same source, but they may have changed due to the personalities of the individuals through which they were transmitted. Or perhaps there are different dialects of angelic language, just as there are in our languages.

All I can say is that I believe that the source of these languages is the Primal Language, and the resemblance in certain cases, even though slight, tends to point to this conclusion.

Fig. 12.3. Henry
Cornelius Agrippa.
Image from *Three Books
of Occult Philosophy,* by
Henry Cornelius Agrippa.

I have studied some of the angelic language of the magus Henry Cornelius Agrippa, who was born in Cologne in 1486 and died in 1535, thus preceding Dr. Dee's angelic communications. Agrippa also claimed to communicate with angels and left samples of his angelic language as well. I did not see any similarities between his angelic language and the Seeress's language, however, although there are similarities between his and John Dee's. Dee had copies of Agrippa's book *Three Books of Occult Philosophy* (printed 1531–1533) when he carried out his angelic conversations. It is possible these influenced Dr. Dee and his angelic language.

It remains a mystery why different mystics, having received the angelic language from angels or spirits, do not always record identical characters. Although we find a few correspondences, this evidence is not sufficient for me to draw a concrete conclusion. I feel this area requires more-extensive research by experts capable of accurately analyzing the material within the languages to determine how one variation of the

The writing called Malachim.

Fig. 12.4. Agrippa's Angelic Language. Image from *Three Books of Occult Philosophy*, by Henry Cornelius Agrippa.

language may have been derived from another and how each may be connected to a primary angelic language. Regarding the primary angelic language and its various interpretations, perhaps you, the reader, will feel drawn to research the subject and be willing and able to extrapolate information others have missed.

13

THE V⊕YNICH
MANUSCRIPT

O ne of the joys of research is that you may come across something
that you were not previously aware of that will be very significant to your work, or at least related in some way. I felt this way when
I first heard of the Voynich manuscript, which is considered the world's
most mysterious manuscript. I recommend a book entitled *The Voynich
Manuscript: The Mysterious Code That Has Defied Interpretation for
Centuries* to get the full story.[1] This is one of the best and most exhaus-
tive treatments on this subject.

The history of the Voynich manuscript began in 1912.[2] Wilfred M.
Voynich was an antiquarian book collector and dealer who traveled the
world searching for and buying rare books and manuscripts. He was
always on the lookout for anything unusual that would bring a fair
price. Little did he know that his next discovery would be the find of
his life and affect many people, both in his lifetime and in the future.

While traveling in Europe, he visited an ancient castle in southern
Italy, where he was allowed to rummage through some old chests. In
them were many beautiful illuminated manuscripts, and one of these
grabbed his attention, standing out from all the rest. Based on the cal-
ligraphy and pigments of the manuscript, he guessed that it was probably written around the thirteenth or fourteenth century. Because of

the nature of the drawings, he believed the manuscript to be a work on natural philosophy or alchemy. It really intrigued him, since he was familiar, as a book collector and dealer, with the script of most languages, and this book was written in a script he could not recognize. He thought this manuscript could be something very significant, so he purchased it from the monastery.

Voynich made copies of the manuscript and sent them to experts all over the world to see if anyone could recognize its language and translate it for him. However, no one could decipher a single word, although most of the experts did feel that the script met the criterion for being a real language. This was based on the structure and repetition of certain characters, something later confirmed by computer analysis. Even though a computer could not translate the characters, it confirmed that their sequence was characteristic of a natural language. This analysis was based on certain word statistics known as Zipf's laws. Since Voynich was not able to succeed in getting it translated or decoded, he decided to sell it.

The manuscript is composed of 116 leaves, or separate pages, of browning vellum inside a blank cover, also made of vellum. Each page is about six inches by nine inches, and the script is very beautiful and written in black ink. There is no indication of an author, date, or any other information about who wrote it, when it was written, or what it is about. There was, however, an old letter attached to it, which we will discuss shortly. There are also many beautiful color illustrations throughout the manuscript. Some of these are drawings of plants; astronomical objects like planets, stars, and suns; anatomical objects; and many unknown and strange-looking objects. It is interesting that some of the drawings look alchemical and others resemble astrological drawings. Most of the plants cannot be linked to any known species on this planet.

It is obvious that someone spent a lot time putting the manuscript together. Many believe it is at least five hundred years old; it is written in a script that no one can identify or decode, and it is illustrated with

Fig. 13.1. A page from the Voynich manuscript. Image courtesy of the Beinecke Rare Book and Manuscript Library at Yale University.

strange drawings that may or may not relate to the text. Even the plants drawn do not resemble any species known on Earth.

It is well known that Leonardo da Vinci had the ability to write in mirror image. He also had a fascination with cryptography and mysterious symbols and writing. Dating experts place the manuscript in the

Fig. 13.2. A strange plant is illustrated in this page from the Voynich manuscript. Image courtesy of the Beinecke Rare Book and Manuscript Library at
Yale University.

second half of the fifteenth century, exactly the time Leonardo lived
(1452–1519). Some researchers think, and the evidence is growing, that
this manuscript may have been written by Leonardo. This is important,
because Leonardo is considered to have been one of the recipients of

this Primal Language. What if this text was written by him in that language or a derivative of that language?

To continue with the story, Voynich found a buyer for the book, one H. P. Krauss, who lived in New York. Krauss was a well-known antiquarian book collector and a one-time president of the prestigious Antiquarian Booksellers Association of America. (I used to attend this convention in New York when Krauss was president but never talked to him about this manuscript.) Krauss paid Voynich $24,500 for the complete manuscript and then tried to resell it for $160,000, but no one would pay this asking price. Instead of selling it, in 1969 he donated it to Yale University, where to this day it is kept in the Beinecke Rare Book and Manuscript Collection, labeled MS 408.

What do we know about its history prior to the time Voynich purchased it? Let's look at some of the possible owners of this most mysterious manuscript.

Many historians are familiar with the Jesuit scholar Athanasius Kircher, who was born in 1602 in Germany, exactly two hundred years before the birth of Frederika Hauffe, the Seeress of Prevorst. What did this monastic have in common with the Seeress of Prevorst?

Kircher has been compared to Leonardo da Vinci, who died about one hundred years before Kircher's birth. Kircher, like Leonardo, was a scholar in many diverse fields. He was noted for his work in Oriental studies, geology, medicine, and Egyptology, and had been one of the first to observe microbes while looking through a microscope. He was several hundred years ahead of his time in suggesting that the plague was caused by microorganisms that infected their host. He has been labeled the last Renaissance Man.

What I found very interesting about Kircher is related to my research on the Great Pyramid of Giza and Egyptology. He was the first to attempt to decipher and translate Egyptian hieroglyphics and is sometimes referred to as the founder of Egyptology. Also, like the Seeress, he claims to have made journeys through higher dimensions. He said he was guided by an angel who called himself Cosmiel. In the middle of the seventeenth century, Kircher published books and drawings reflecting his understanding of the metaphysical world. Many modern metaphysical beliefs and philosophies have their foundation in his ideas. For example, he said that everything is based on a perfect octave: "The world consisted of a perfect harmony, namely, from the earth to the starry heavens is a perfect octave." G. I. Gurdjieff (1877–1949) later founded his teachings on the law of the octave. Kircher was also the first to illustrate and provide descriptions of the first Magic Lantern (which was similar to our modern-day slide projectors). Instead of slides, pictures were painted on glass and candles were used as lights to project an image on the wall.

In 1639, when Kircher was thirty-seven, he received a strange and mysterious letter from a Georg Baresch, who lived in Prague. Baresch had written to Kircher asking for his help. It seems that an unusual book had fallen into his hands that he could not decipher. This book was illustrated with many strange pictures of botanical, astronomical, and alchemical objects, and it had been written in a script that Baresch had never seen before. Indeed, no one knew its language. Baresch had copies made of some of the pages, which he sent to Kircher, but unfortunately Kircher told him that he could not decipher the script or glean any information from the pages.

We do have a few clues, however, of the manuscript's history from a letter that was attached to it.

This letter was dated 1665 and was from Johannes Marcus Marci to Athanasius Kircher, making the manuscript a gift to him. Marci, who lived in Prague, explained to Kircher that he had inherited the manuscript from his close friend Georg Baresch, who, up until the time of his death, had been trying to decipher the manuscript. (Apparently Marci kept the manuscript for several years before sending it to Kircher. Maybe he was attempting to decode it himself but, frustrated, ultimately gave up.)

Thus we know the ownership of this manuscript passed from Georg Baresch to Johannes Marcus Marci to Athanasius Kircher. We do not know what happened to it after Kircher received it, and in fact do not have any proof that Kircher actually received it from Marci, except for this letter. The scholars are split on the issue, but to me the evidence is compelling that Kircher did receive it but never told anyone about it. I believe this manuscript was the Voynich manuscript.

Let's explore one statement that Kircher made. He said he couldn't decipher the script or make out anything about it. We must ask ourselves whether Kircher was telling Baresch the truth. Kircher was only thirty-seven years old at the time, and this was several decades before he published any of his metaphysical works and ideas. Was it possible that he actually *was* able to decode this manuscript and thus have access to its metaphysical knowledge, knowledge that no one else had? Did this manuscript give him the key to the Primal Language?

As mentioned, he claimed to be able to communicate with an angel and enter into higher dimensions. Later, when he published his works on this, everyone would assume that he arrived at this knowledge and these abilities by himself. If he had been able to decode the Voynich manuscript, then, it would make sense that he might keep his findings secret and not want anyone to know about his discovery. Also, like Leonardo, Kircher was the inventor of many incredible and futuristic devices. Could it be that Leonardo recorded, in cipher, information about this Primal Language, information that would eventually find its way into the hands of a worthy recipient who would be successful in decoding it?

It appears Kircher was in that line of successors. Baresch did not have the ability to decode it and acted as a middleman or courier to get it to the proper person. Was it by chance or destiny that he sent it to Kircher?

Kircher died in 1680, and whatever happened to this manuscript after his death until it appeared again in the Villa Mondragone is anybody's guess.

I compared the language of the Voynich manuscript with that of the Seeress's drawings. The Voynich script does not seem to be similar to the Seeress's inner language, but some of the diagrams have a similarity,

Fig. 13.3. An unusual plant found on a page in the Voynich manuscript. Image courtesy of the Beinecke Rare Book and Manuscript Library, Yale University.

Fig. 13.4. A cryptic illustration from the Voynich manuscript. Image courtesy of the Beinecke Rare Book and Manuscript Library, Yale University.

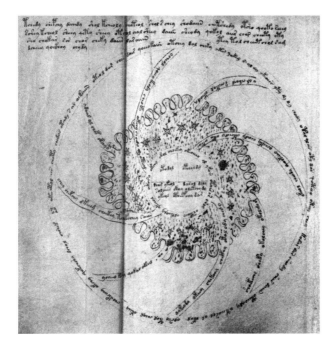

Fig. 13.5. Some aspects of this circle, found in the Voynich manuscript, are not unlike circles drawn by the Seeress. Image courtesy of the Beinecke Rare Book and Manuscript Library, Yale University.

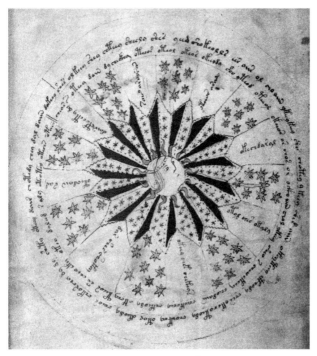

Fig. 13.6. Another page from the Voynich manuscript. Image courtesy of the Beinecke Rare Book and Manuscript Library, Yale University.

especially to her Circles. I have been studying the Voynich manuscript, and the possibility that Leonardo wrote it is extremely interesting. I think the key to solving it is the base-7 of the Seeress's numerical system. The number seven keeps coming up in the diagrams of the Voynich manuscript, and I think this is a clue. I believe I am the first to propose that the key to deciphering the Voynich manuscript is based on sevens. I know that seven is a spiritual number and significant to mystical thought; it's not unusual to find this number in the diagrams and symbols of many works on mysticism. Even the stars drawn by Hildegard of Bingen in "The Cosmic Egg" show the seven patterns.*

Also, I believe that the illustrations on each page of the manuscript play a part in decoding the characters on that specific page. Whether it was designed to be used as a template or some other tool has yet to be determined. Currently I am working on finding more similarities between these two mysterious works and trying to decode the Voynich manuscript using a base-7 system.

In talking about the manuscript with some of the curators and staff at Yale University, I asked if any ultraviolet or infrared studies had been done. This is important, since it could reveal an underlying painting or diagram. It might also reveal whether the manuscript had been doctored or modified from the original. I was told that those studies had been done and nothing unusual had been found. Someone else did tell me that he had never heard that they had been done, but he may not have been in a position to know about them if they had been.[3] If such studies were in fact done, the results should be published.

There is also a long line of speculation that Dr. John Dee was at one time an owner of this manuscript. The evidence is not completely convincing but is worth mentioning, because Dee also claimed to be able to write and speak in the language of the angels. In one of his diaries,

---

*Hildegard of Bingen was an eleventh-century German abbess, artist, and author whose artwork reflects her cosmic vision. In one drawing, the entire universe is represented as a cosmic egg, the egg being the symbol of life. The surrounding flames signify the omnipresence of God.

Dee refers to a book in his library that he called *Songa*. Dee supposedly spent much time attempting to decipher this book but was unable to do so, and many believe that this was the Voynich manuscript. Also, Dee was an expert on ciphers and sometimes acted as a spy for Queen Elizabeth I. Thus it would make sense that, as a cryptologist and a mystic, he would be interested in something like this. He would also have the means and contacts to obtain a book such as the Voynich manuscript. Unfortunately, this is just speculation, with very little evidence to support it.

Where do we go from here? I'm always asked that question when I'm interviewed about my research. I think we need more cryptologists to study this manuscript, and more testing needs to be done. I believe the key to deciphering it is the base-7 system, with the illustrations playing some role.

So what is my conclusion about the Voynich manuscript and the Seeress's inner language? I cannot find any strong similarities, except for their interesting circular drawings; more research needs to be done in comparing them. The divisions, the stars, and the symbols do seem to have something in common, and I bring this to the attention of the reader to encourage further research and comparisons.[4]

I hope more studies will be done and that we find additional clues about the meaning, origin, and purpose of the Voynich manuscript. It is the world's most mysterious book.

14

THE DEATH
OF THE SEERESS

In May 1828, the Seeress said that something remarkable would happen to her, but she didn't know exactly what it would be. She told Dr. Kerner that she could no longer move backward and forward in her Sun Sphere, as she had been able to do before. Also, the specific point in her Life Sphere, which she should not have reached until December, had suddenly sprung forward. This indicated to her that her time on Earth was limited, and possibly that death was approaching. This seemed to be confirmed when her protecting spirit appeared to her and pointed to a half-open coffin. She interpreted this as signifying either approaching death or that something perilous would occur.

In January 1829, she said that the months of her current Sun Sphere would last only until May 2, instead of until December 27, as they should have done (see figures 14.1 and 14.3). By this loss, she was thrust out of these months, and she came to believe that she was going to die in May. Then, in the middle of the month, she lost the sensation of all her spheres and said that her seven Sun Spheres had fallen from her. This obviously was not a good sign and was yet another confirmation that her end was rapidly approaching. On May 2, she fell into a

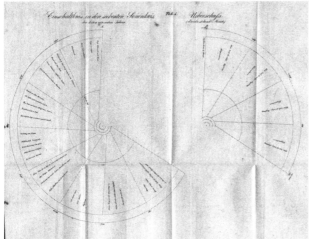

Fig. 14.1. Sun Circle of the Seeress in her last year. Image from *Die Seherin von Prevorst: Eröffnungen über das innere Leben des Menschen und über das Hereinragen einer Geisterwelt in die unsere*.

Fig. 14.2. English translation of figure 14.1. Translated by and courtesy of George Setian.

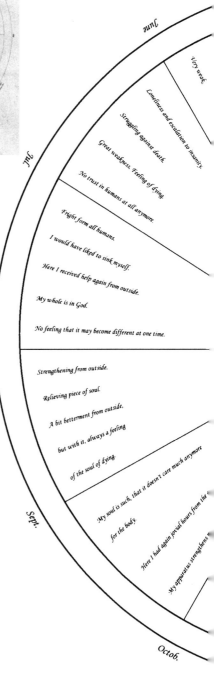

June

Very weak.

Loneliness and exaltation to insanity.

Struggling against death.

Great weakness. Feeling of dying.

July

No trust in humans at all anymore.

Fright form all humans.

I would have liked to sink myself.

Here I received help again from outside.

My whole is in God.

No feeling that it may become different at one time.

Aug.

Strengthening from outside.

Relieving piece of soul.

A bit betterment from outside,

but with it, always a feeling

of the soul of dying.

Sept.

My soul is such, that it doesn't care much anymore for the body.

Here I had again jovial hours from the

My apparatus strengthens

Octob.

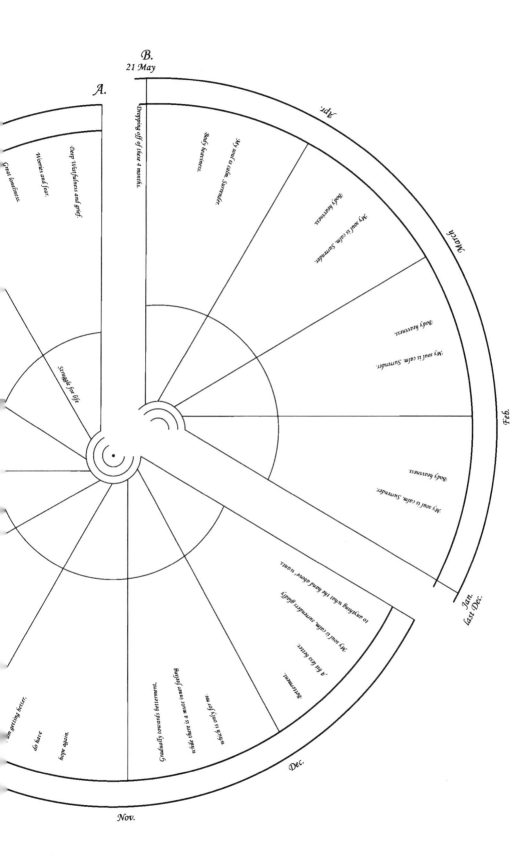

B.
21 May

A.

Great loneliness.

Worries and fear.

Deep Watfulness and grief.

Dropping off of these 4 months.

Body faintness.

My soul is calm. Surrender.

Apr.

Body heaviness.

My soul is calm. Surrender.

March

Body heaviness.

My soul is calm. Surrender.

Feb.

Body heaviness.

My soul is calm. Surrender.

Jan.
last Dec.

Struggle for life

to anything what the hand above wants.

My soul is calm, surrenders gladly

A bit less better.

Betterment.

Gradually towards betterment.

while there is a mute inner feeling

which is only for me.

am getting better.

do have

hope again.

Dec.

Nov.

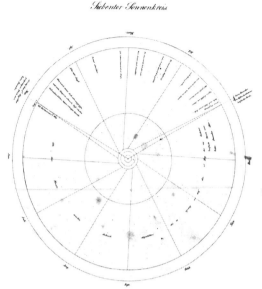

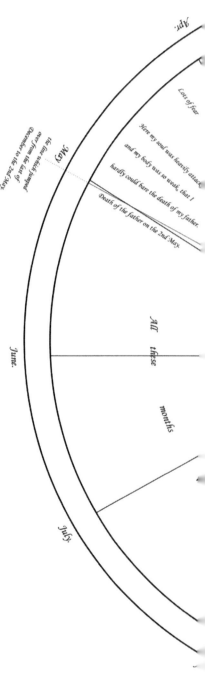

Fig. 14.3. Another rendition of the Sun Circle of the Seeress in her last year. Image from *Die Seherin von Prevorst: Eröffnungen über das innere Leben des Menschen und über das Hereinragen einer Geisterwelt in die unsere.*

Fig. 14.4. English translation of figure 14.3. Translated by and courtesy of George Setian.

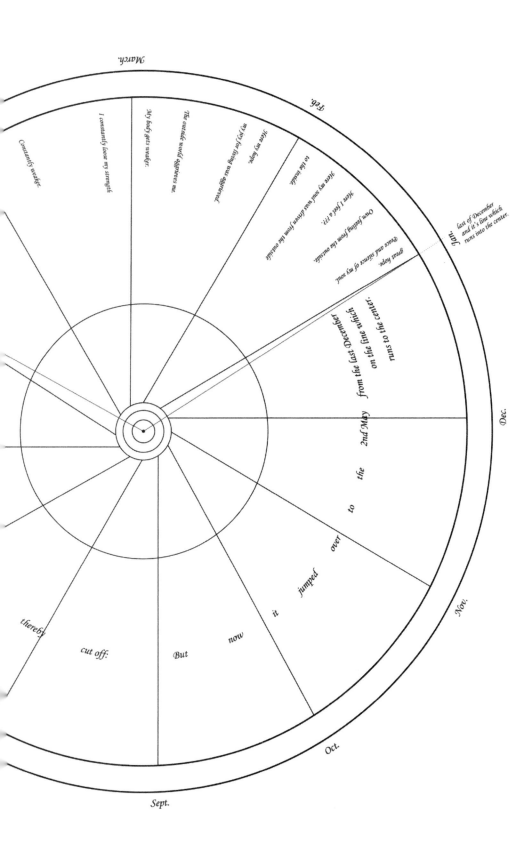

clairvoyant dream in which she spoke aloud, as was typical:

> I am on a mountain—Oh! Might I go down to the right, over those
> golden clouds, where I see that flowery vale! To the left I see noth-
> ing but graves and corruption—behind me I see mankind struggling
> and fighting, like lions and tigers—to the right the flowers are smil-
> ing on me, but I will to death and the grave. Must I fall under this
> stroke? Lead me where thou wilt—Oh! Fearful dream!—Oh! Guide
> me! Must I sink into the abyss? Thou art powerful and strong—Do
> I understand thee aright? —Must I remain on this mountain? Yes,
> I must stay till the hour is come; but thou art with me by day and
> night—if thou forsakest me, I fall. Oh! Let me awake from this fear-
> ful dream![1]

She said that she had now entered a new clairvoyant state, deeper
than any state she had ever been in. We do not have a description of
this state as, for some reason, she would not describe what she saw. She
said that her body was dead but alive, and that her soul was more free
and calmer than ever: "Let my body be no more regarded—be no care
taken of it; 'tis a torn garment, that I no longer value—into thy hand, O
Lord! I commit my spirit."[2] This was the presentiment of her approaching death, and she maintained an attitude of indifference toward it,
which is what she recommended for everyone at such a time.

She requested to be brought back to her home in Lowenstein, but
Dr. Kerner was not in favor of this because of her very weak condition.
He finally relented, and on May 5, 1829, she returned to Lowenstein.
After she arrived there, she fell into a condition that resembled that of
a dying person. Three weeks before she died, she had three visions of
her approaching death.

In the first, a female form taller than herself, enveloped in black,
appeared to her. She could see only the feet of this figure, as the rest
of it was draped in black. The figure stood in an open coffin, and
beside it was a white cross. The apparition beckoned the Seeress, and

she felt its cold breath. She said it was not a spirit, but a "portentous second-sight."

Three days before the Seeress died, she raised three of her fingers, as if taking an oath, and declared that her life could scarcely endure three days longer. She told Dr. Kerner that two spirits, which had just visited her, had answered her inquiry as to why they had come. They said to her, "You are already of us."[3] This was her second vision.

In her third vision, she told Dr. Kerner that her deceased father had just visited her. This was interesting, since her father had been dead for a year, and she had never had a visit from him in the spirit form. She asked him why he had not revealed himself to her before, and he said that it had not been in his power to reveal himself earlier. Unfortunately, she was too sick to be able to carry on any lengthy conversations at this time. She was very desirous of communicating some revelations that her father had given her concerning the spirit world, as well as her Sun Sphere and inner calculations, but she was not able to do so. What a shame this information is lost to the world. What new spiritual secrets would she have revealed to us?

The night before her death, Dr. Kerner saw her in a dream with two other female forms. (Kerner had no idea that she was so close to death.) In this dream, she appeared to be perfectly recovered.

On August 5, 1829, she became delirious but was still in a very pious state of mind. She requested that hymns be sung to her. She often called loudly for Dr. Kerner, who was not present.

At ten o'clock, her sister saw a tall, bright form enter the chamber, and at the same instant the Seeress uttered a loud cry of joy, as if she were being set free. After a short interval, her soul also departed, leaving behind an unrecognizable body. Not a single trace of her former features remained. During her life, her countenance was of the sort that is borrowed wholly from the spirit within. It is therefore not surprising that when the spirit departed, the face was no longer the same. The body was found to be wasted to a skeleton.

On August 8, 1829, the remains of the Seeress of Prevorst were deposited in the idyllic churchyard of Lowenstein, where the body of her grandmother and grandfather lay. Thus ended the life of one of the world's greatest mystics, clairvoyants, and spiritualists. She was a true Seeress in every sense of the word.

After her death, she appeared to her oldest sister seven times. Kerner knew the details of these appearances, but because her family was still alive when he wrote his book, he did not feel the time was right to disclose the information.

It is very significant and fortunate that during the Seeress's life, Dr. Kerner allowed other experts and professionals access to her. She was studied and observed by the leading philosophers, doctors, metaphysicians, and occult experts in Germany. Very few clairvoyants have been subjected to such detailed scrutiny and evaluation. Granted, scientific study in the nineteenth century was not as advanced and sophisticated as it is today, but it was as complete and thorough as it could be at that time. In fact, this may be the best-documented case of a clairvoyant on

Fig. 14.5. The grave of the Seeress. Image from *Die Seherin von Prevorst und die Botschaft Justinus Kerner,* by Justinus Kerner and von Felix Kretschmar.

record. She passed the experts' tests and was acknowledged as being a true Seeress who could enter the spirit world.

Let's sum up some of her paranormal abilities that were acknowledged by Kerner and his associates.

- She was able to communicate directly with spirits. She could both see and hear them and sense their presence when they were near.
- She was able to speak and write in an inner language, which she claimed was the language of the spirits.
- She knew the "inner mathematics" of all things and events. She was able to calculate the number that all people carry with them and take with them after they die.
- She constructed diagrams (Circles) that represented both the inner and outer worlds. She could even predict events using these circles.
- She could both diagnose and prescribe for individuals when in her clairvoyant state. Many of her treatments were based on the patient's inner number. She also used amulets and paper with inner language written on it.
- She had an extreme spiritual sensitivity to inanimate objects, including metals, gems, minerals, colored stones, glass, sand, crystals, and water. She had a high level of sensitivity to colors, sounds, and the sun and moon.
- She had precognition and could predict events in the near future.
- At times, the laws of gravity were suspended around her, and she was observed in a state of levitation.

A very interesting point is that her speaking in the language of the spirits could have been the beginning of what the charismatic movement now calls "speaking in tongues."

Please keep in mind that the Seeress never claimed infallibility. She was observing and experiencing the spiritual world through the filters in her body and her mind. Even if she was able to experience the higher worlds directly, her mind wouldn't necessarily have the capacity to be 100 percent accurate in interpreting and then describing everything she had been privy to.

I'd like to quote the statement by Dr. Kerner that he included at the end of the first part of his book on the Seeress.

> Go ye into the world, my reader; and if the former part of this book be not to your mind, trouble yourself with it no more—go ye into the world, which will tell you that all this is deception, or the effects of a diseased imagination; but wait till the still, midnight hour finds you at the bed-side of the dying, or till the parting hymn is sung by the grave of your well-beloved. The tumult of the world drowns the voice of our sweet mother, nature; but the time comes at last, when the wheels stop—the clamor ceases—and that loving voice strikes in full accord upon our hearts; and then we stand amazed, that all our life long such a chorus of heavenly harmonies had been calling to us, and we heard them not.[4]

> Beloved, when you read these pages, although you be yet in the flower of youth, remember that life flies like a dream; and when it is gone, what will avail all the knowledge you have acquired as a means to honor and fame? You believe in a future state, but think little of the way that leads to it. You turn away your eyes from the picture of old age that awaits you, and seek to drown the warning voice within, by the distractions of the world without. But you cannot silence it, for it is the voice of God; and do what you will, it will yet cry to you, in the midst of pleasures, "Thou must die!" And when death threatens, you cling to the weak science of man, and rest dearer hopes on an apothecary's draught, than on all the treasures of the world.[5]

15

DR. KERNER AND HIS
INNER CIRCLE

The world owes a great debt to Dr. Justinus Kerner, physician to the Seeress. The Seeress never wrote a book or an article herself, and in fact we have very little from her own hand. How, then, do we know so much about her life, her revelations, and her inner language? It is because of Dr. Kerner. He, in a sense, acted as a scribe for the Seeress. He faithfully recorded her statements, the important events that occurred around her, and anything else related to her mystical states. He was smart enough to realize that what was going on with the Seeress would be of interest to others, both in his time and in the future; he had great foresight.

He also knew in his heart that he would eventually write a book about the Seeress. It was standard at that time, as is true today, for a doctor who discovered something new to publish and thereby make his findings known. He was a true believer in the Seeress and felt that the information about her would benefit humankind in that it would produce spiritual enlightenment in people exposed to her story. He did not do it to make money, and, in fact, he probably made very little from the sales of his books. As a famous physician in Germany, he was well off and didn't need an income from book royalties. It was out of dedication that he wrote a book and published it.

With this said, it is important if not imperative to look at the life of

Dr. Kerner and examine why he was so interested in the Seeress. Also, who were his inner circle of mystics, as some have called them? What were their relationships with the Seeress, and what did they say about her? There are few published works about Dr. Kerner. The best source for his life is *Pioneers of the Spiritual Reformation,* a very difficult book to find.[1]

Dr. Kerner could best be described as a physician, scientist, artist, poet, lover of nature, and someone with a great interest in spirituality and metaphysics. He was a Renaissance man in the true sense of the term. As mentioned, many people believe that his book on the Seeress, first published in 1829[2] and translated by Catherine Crowe in 1845,[3] paved the way, in people's minds, for the reception of modern spiritualism when the Fox sisters came along in 1848. In Howitt's *History of the Supernatural,*[4] Kerner is described as "the most prominent figure in the spiritual circle of Germany." How did Dr. Kerner go from a traditional medical doctor who was at best skeptical of the clairvoyant ability of the Seeress to a true believer?

Justinus Kerner was born on September 18, 1786, in the bustling town of Ludwigsburg, Germany. He was the youngest of six children. His family was well off. His father was well educated and was employed as a government official. His mother was a very gentle person who loved her children. In 1795, at the age of nine, a great change occurred in Kerner's life. The family decided to move to the abbey of Maulbronn because Kerner's father had accepted a position as bailiff there.

The abbey was just the opposite of Ludwigsburg. It was surrounded by woods, vineyards, lakes, and ponds. This very rural area was the perfect place for a child to develop a love for nature. Justinus attended the abbey school but was not all that interested in the studies of languages, geography, or arithmetic it offered. Nature alone absorbed his attention. He enjoyed working with his father in the garden and had an intense desire to learn everything he could about plants and animals. He also developed keen powers of observation, which would come in handy years later.

Because of the threat of French troops marching into the area where they were living, his parents decided to send him back to Ludwigsburg for safety. Within a short time of his return there, he developed a severe illness that produced in him an extraordinary excitability of the nerves of the stomach; this lasted almost an entire year. It was during this time that he arrived at an important insight that may have affected him for the rest of his life. As he was studying the metamorphoses of beetles and butterflies, the idea came to him that as the chrysalis state exists between the grub and the butterfly, a similar "middle-state" must also exist for human beings after death.

Another interesting aspect of this illness was how he was treated for it. The prescriptions of his physician—pills and mixtures—had no effect on him. One day, he happened to come upon a well-known and celebrated magnetizer, Gmelin of Heilbronn. Gmelin made several "passes" over Kerner, and shortly afterward Kerner recovered speedily from his illness.

It's fascinating that he attributed his recovery to mesmerism, given the fact that when he first met the Seeress, he wanted nothing to do with the therapy of magnetism. Is it also possible that this experience awakened him to the spiritual world, due to the fact that after this event he had presentiments and prophetic dreams? The first of these prophetic dreams occurred immediately after he was magnetized by Gmelin, and he recorded it in one of his books, which is entitled *Picture Book of My Childhood*. In the dream he beheld the images of some of his future friends and even his future wife. He also said that these dreams arose from the pit of his stomach. (Remember, the pit of the stomach was where a closed book would be placed for a clairvoyant to "read.") Also, we have mentioned that psychic ability runs in families but sometimes skips generations. In later years, Kerner's grandmother on his father's side also had prophetic dreams. He and his grandmother obviously had a close spiritual connection.

As Kerner grew up, he tried various occupations, including carpentry, working as a merchant in a cloth-manufacturing plant, and being a copyist, which did not appeal to him at all; he found it boring and unrewarding. After several years of it, a professor and friend who lived at Tübingen procured a scholarship for Kerner at Tübingen University. He also invited him into his house to live while a student. So in the autumn of 1804, at the age of eighteen, Kerner entered Tübingen University. Just before entering the town, he had a prophetic dream in which it was revealed to him what he should study and become. He entered that university town saying to himself, "Thou must become a physician."[5] He remained four years at Tübingen University, and in addition to medicine, he studied natural sciences, classical literature, philology (the study of languages and literature), and *belles lettres* (poetry, fiction, essays, and drama, valued more for their aesthetic appeal than their practicality; in French, this term means fine or beautiful letters or writing). He completed his four years of study in the autumn of 1808 but remained in Tübingen for a few more months to complete his doctor's thesis.

Karl August Varnhagen von Ense, who associated with Kerner during his student years, recalls that one night they were reading Jung-Stilling's *Theory of Spiritual Communication* together. He said this about Kerner: "His eyes have something peculiarly spiritual and pious in their glance—all that is magically magnetic is to be met in him to an extraordinary degree."[6] Here again is another example of Kerner's interest and influence in the spiritual and psychic world at an early age.

Why did he seem to reject all this later in life? My guess is that when he became a practicing physician, he had to conform to the attitudes and customs of current medical practice. Most physicians looked down on anything paranormal and lumped it in the category of imagination and mental illness. Perhaps Kerner simply conformed to the views of his peers and suppressed all his experiences and beliefs in the supernatural until the Seeress came along. She reignited the spiritual life in him.

In 1808, Kerner left Tübingen to begin his career as a physician. When he was twenty-one, he married a poor girl. His friends called this an act of folly, but he knew he was meant to marry her: she was the girl he had seen many years earlier in his prophetic dream.

Kerner immediately set forth on a journey through Germany to explore the country and look for a place to practice medicine. The following year he settled down in Wildbad, in the midst of the Black Forest. He practiced medicine there for a time and then moved to Welzheim, where "a more considerable practice presented itself."[7] His first child was a daughter born to him and his wife, Frederika, whom he called Rickele. It is interesting to note that while in Welzheim, Kerner made several acquaintances, one of whom was a blind man named Melchoir Lang, who was endowed with the natural gift of healing. Thus Kerner was able to observe and experience the phenomenon of healing directly through his friend.

It was at Welzheim that he gained a national reputation by studying individuals who had been poisoned by sausages that had spoiled. In 1820 he published the first complete description of botulism, which was a clinically accurate study. Until Kerner drew attention to it, this disease had never been scientifically investigated. What is interesting is that when he published his report, under the title "New Observations Regarding the Frequent Deadly Poisonings in Württemburg Through the Consumption of Smoked Sausages," he added how in the Middle Ages, the kings of France possessed the gift of healing goiter through "laying on of hands" and pronouncing the well-known words *"Le Roi touché, Dieu te guerisse"*: the King touches, and God heals you.

In January 1819, Kerner settled in Weinsberg in the position of district physician, to which he was appointed by the government. Weinsberg at that time was scarcely more than a village of vine growers, and not very accessible. In 1822, at the foot of the hill of the Weibertreu Castle, Kerner built a house for himself and his family; here he would spend the rest of his life. Shortly after moving into the new home, his third and last child was born.

In 1826, Kerner published the first of his series of works connected with the inner life of human beings. It was entitled *The History of Two Somnambulists: Together with Certain Other Notable Things from the Realms of Magical Cure and Psychology*. This book was the actual diary kept by Kerner while treating two very remarkable patients. One was a young girl, the daughter of a vine grower in Weinsberg. The other was a young woman who had been born in Stuttgart but later moved to Weinsberg. Each exhibited supernatural abilities and was treated magnetically by Dr. Kerner; both were eventually restored to health.

As word got out that Kerner was treating individuals using magnetic therapy, people from nearby districts swarmed to him to ask for his help. Even patients who claimed they were possessed and haunted came to see him for his magnetic cures. Some years later, when the Seeress of Prevorst appeared, he refused to give her any magnetic therapy. Why the change? Was it because he became overwhelmed with this and no longer wished to be known as a doctor who healed magnetically? Did he feel he should return to the traditional side of medicine only, completely abandoning his work as a magnetizer? We may never know the answer to these questions, but it is interesting to contemplate his dramatic change of attitude in such a short period.

Shortly after the 1826 publication of Kerner's *The History of Two Somnambulists,* Frederika Hauffe was brought from Prevorst to Weinsberg to be under his care. Kerner, believing that it was his duty to procure other opinions, allowed others to investigate her condition. Soon his home was visited by many of the best-known doctors, scientists, and philosophers in Germany.

One such person was David Strauss, the author of *Life of Jesus.* He was at that time "orthodox in his religious views"[8] but acknowledged nonetheless the ability of the Seeress. Years later, Strauss said that when he first met the Seeress, he could not remember a comparable moment. He said when he laid his hand in hers, he knew his whole life would lie open to her. He said he felt as if the ground had been pulled out from under him and he was sinking into an abyss.

Another visitor and observer was Professor Adolph Karl August von Eschenmayer (1768–1852), of Tübingen. He became very close to Kerner when investigating the Seeress and was convinced of her clairvoyant ability. Eschenmayer wrote about her in his book *Mysteries.*

Kerner also recruited a group of mystics to study her revelations and make them known. This group had discovered similarities in her revelations to the teachings of Plato and Pythagoras. They also published their own journal.

In addition to his book on the life of the Seeress, in 1831 Dr. Kerner started publishing a periodical entitled *Leaves from Prevorst; or, Original Literary Fruits for Lovers of the Inner Life*. Others who helped in publishing this periodical were Professor Eschenmayer; Frederik von Meyer, of Frankfurt; Gotthilf Heinrich von Schubert; Guido Gorres; and Franz von Baader. Between 1831 and 1839, twelve volumes were published. Kerner developed such a close relationship with Schubert and Meyer that he dedicated the first edition of *The Seeress of Prevorst* to these individuals, whom he called his "worthy and honorable friends."

In 1834, Kerner's book *History of Modern Cases of Possession, Together with Observations Made in the Realm of Kako-demoniac, Magnetic Appearances* was published. This was followed in 1836 by the publication entitled *Letter to the Superior-Medical-Counsellor Schelling, Concerning the Appearance of Possession: Demoniacal, Magnetic Suffering and Its Cure Through Magnetic Treatment as Known to the Ancients.*

Fig. 15.1. Karl August Eschenmayer. Image from *Die Seherin von Prevorst und die Botschaft Justinus Kerner*, by Justinus Kerner and von Felix Kretschmar.

Fig. 15.2. Gotthilf Heinrich Schubert. Image from *Die Seherin von Prevorst und die Botschaft Justinus Kerner,* by Justinus Kerner and von Felix Kretschmar.

Fig. 15.3. Johann Friedrich von Meyer. Image from *Die Seherin von Prevorst und die Botschaft Justinus Kerner,* by Justinus Kerner and von Felix Kretschmar.

It's very interesting that Kerner not only promoted magnetic treatment but also claimed that its practice went back to ancient times. What a change in attitude! In 1839, he wrote *Leaves from Prevorst* and established another periodical of larger size entitled *Magikon, or Archives for Observations Concerning the Realms of the Spirit-World and of Magnetic Life.* This periodical continued until 1853. In 1849, he wrote an autobiography of his early years entitled *Picture Book of My Childhood.* He followed these up with other publications that documented the appearance of spirits.

Unfortunately, around 1840 he noticed a decrease in his visual ability. He had started to develop a cataract. Cataracts were not easily treated at that time, and most people went blind from them although if one formed only in one eye, some ability to see was retained. In Kerner's case, he was able to continue to write and pursue his medical practice.

In the 1850s, "table turning" was very much in the news in Germany and of interest to many. Kerner published a pamphlet in 1853 entitled *Somnambulic Tables; or, the History and Explanation of That Phenomenon*. In it, he ascribes this phenomenon to an undiscovered or measured fluid, neither magnetic nor electrical, but perhaps related to both. He said the Seeress of Prevorst claimed that this fluid came from the "spirit of the nerves." Kerner was fascinated with Mesmer, and his last publication, in 1856, was entitled *Franz Anton Mesmer, the Discoverer of Animal Magnetism, with Recollections of Him, etc.*

Kerner's wife, Rickele, died in 1854, and he then was taken care of by his children and grandchildren. He was offered a pension by the king of Württemberg and later by Ludwig of Bavaria, which enabled him to live comfortably until his death. He suffered from blindness and a nervous condition during his last days and died of influenza on February 21, 1862. His last words were, "Lord, Thy work is accomplished! Good night, Good night, may you all sleep well."[9] At his funeral, he did not want any oration or ceremony. He wanted a simple burial with only a flat stone with his name and his wife's name on it, marked with the simple inscription "Frederika Kerner and Her Justinus."

We can't estimate how many people have been influenced and changed spiritually as a result of Dr. Kerner's book on the Seeress of Prevorst, but one such person was Carl Jung. Few know that Carl Jung held spiritual séances. He started experimenting with séances around the year 1895 with his cousin Helly. Jung was about twenty years old at the time, and Helly was about fifteen. She had mediumistic abilities, claimed to have visits from her dead grandfather, and had even traveled in the spirit world. On Helly's fifteenth birthday, Jung gave her a copy of Kerner's *The Seeress of Prevorst* (German edition). This book caused her to enter a strong spontaneous trance. (Here is another example of the spiritual power of this book.) These séances with Helly continued on and off for many years.

Years later, Jung said that these séances with Helly contained the origin of all his ideas. He used the Seeress of Prevorst as the model for his medium, Helly. We know how much Carl Jung has influenced our world.

16

FINAL THOUGHTS AND SPECULATIONS

From studying the history of the Primal Language, it appears that a person may obtain this language in at least three ways.

1. *Received directly from God or the angels.* This is how Adam, or the first human, received this language, according to the tradition of the Kabbalah. The Bible stories seem to confirm that he had knowledge of this language by his naming of the animals and having power over them. It appears that Dr. John Dee also obtained the angelic language directly from the angels.

2. *Transmitted or passed on from one person to another.* In chapter 1, using the Bible as a source, we have tried to trace how this language could have been passed down from one person to the next, and established a possible chain of recipients. Secret societies may also have preserved and passed down the language to their select inner core of initiates. I believe that because it was being passed from one person to another over a long period, many errors and distortions crept in. A new dispensation would be necessary and would be given by God, the angels, or a messenger (as in number 1 above). As with any knowledge or teaching, the true meaning of the language may have been lost over time; thus a new messenger would be needed to return its original meaning to the world.

3. *Revealed to us from our own inner being.* The Seeress clearly said that this information is latent in all of us and needs only to be awakened and then developed. It appears this is how the Seeress received this knowledge. This is good news, since there is the potential for this knowledge to be awakened in all of humanity.

I also mentioned previously that the angelic language and the language of the spirits are the same language. The Seeress had said that her inner language was the language of Jacob of the Bible, the original language of humankind, so we know she is referring to the Primal Language or language of the angels. Variations may be produced in this angelic language by the way it is communicated from the spirit world to the physical plane. The person receiving it acts as a filter and, since each person is different, the information may be colored by the level of his or her spiritual development and personality. Just as a medium can transfer information from the spirit world only through his or her physical body and mind, the recipient of angelic communication may cloud or distort the message as it passes into his or her physical body and mind. Thus the process is not a perfect one, and the recipient may cause variations and distortions. That's why there are differences between the angelic language of the Seeress and those of John Dee, Henry Cornelius Agrippa, and others.

There also appear to be similarities among the languages of different mystics and seers. I believe we will eventually recover or decipher the base or original angelic language from which all these others were derived. Researchers are trying to find a basic script that all these variations came from. This is not an easy task, since the scripts, as you have seen, are very complicated and not things we are familiar with.

I would also like to emphasize that even if we could decipher the language code of the Seeress's inner language, the key is how the words are actually pronounced, and I don't know how we would be able to discover that. As mentioned before, we need the actual sound vibration, for the sound is the magic and carries the power to transform things. Just as in the King's Chamber of the Great Pyramid, resonance is the key. Language experts are needed to analyze and decode this script. I hope eventually to try computer analysis, but the language pattern may not lend itself to this, given the inordinately large number of variables that must be taken into account.

I had an interesting idea as I was contemplating the key to this language. What if the script of the Seeress's inner language is based on a three-dimensional template or object (or even a higher dimension) projecting itself onto a two-dimensional, flat plane to produce the script? For example, if you take a 3-D object like a ball and pass it through a 2-D plane, a 2-D living being on the plane will initially see a point appear as the ball starts to pass through its flat world, then a small circle will appear, which would grow larger and larger as the ball moves through the plane; then the circle will get smaller and smaller after the ball passes halfway through the surface. Then it will shrink to a point, and finally disappear as the ball passes completely through the surface of the plane. A more complicated 3-D object passing through this 2-D plane would produce a variety of strange shapes.

Also, what if the 3-D object could rotate and change its position as it passed through the 2-D plane? This would create an almost infinite variety of patterns. In college, I read the book *Flatland,*[1] which gives examples of this. So my idea is that as the 3-D template moved through a 2-D plane, it would produce different symbols, which would be the letter system. If we knew the original shape of the 3-D object, we would know how all the letters would be produced as it passed through a plane in a specific orientation. In fact, the shape could be in a dimension higher than the third, but it would be beyond our ability to visualize anything that complicated. Could this 3-D object be the original Word of God, that is, the original vibration or the OM point that produced the entire universe? Could a higher-dimensional object, by projecting itself onto our 3-D world, produce sound and vibrations, and could this have been the WORD of creation? Was this the big bang?

Picture God's thoughts creating this multidimensional form. They materialize and move into the physical universe, leaving a trail, like a 3-D object passing through a 2-D plane. As a divine thought moves through, it produces sound vibrations, which create matter and energy. The original language, both written and spoken, is based on this form. Vibrating strings of energy, as proposed in string theory, would be the debris it leaves behind, which creates the matter and energy of our universe. Thus, if we can reconstruct this form, at least its 3-D representation, this would show us how the 2-D inner language of the Seeress was formed.

We would also want to be able to pronounce this language. As mentioned, I'm not sure how we could figure this out unless we can uncover some additional information, maybe from mystics. We can also look at other possible angelic or unknown manuscripts that may be derived from this inner language, such as the Voynich manuscript.

Another way to visualize what I am talking about is to picture this object as a comet. As it moves, it leaves a debris trail, which would be the strings from string theory. As they form, they create all the matter and energy of the universe. Also, a time factor is involved. Does the object pass through slowly or rapidly? Does it mutate or change shape with time? Maybe the time factor affects the sound it will make, as in the case of a fast- or slow-moving train. If the object passes quickly, the sound would be high-pitched; and if slowly, it would have a lower frequency. Many variables are involved.

So where do we go from here? We work with what we have. We have the Seeress's diagrams and scripts. We have other angelic languages. We need to feed these into a computer to see if it can re-create a 3-D object that would produce all these 2-D figures as it passes through a plane. This isn't an easy task. Also, there may be a simpler explanation that we're missing.

I'd now like to mention an interesting similarity I found between the Seeress's script and something that appears to be totally unrelated. I have been interested in UFOs since I was in high school. I have never been a full-fledged UFO researcher, but I do believe there is something to it. Many of the sightings are not of conventional aircraft or objects. I have been especially interested in the alleged crash of a UFO in Roswell, New Mexico, in 1947. The government at that time claimed that it was a weather balloon that had crashed, and that the debris that was recovered was a radar reflector. Of course, the government has always denied that it was a UFO.

Ufologists have continued to insist that this is a cover-up, that there was a real UFO crash, and debris from this craft was recovered and is hidden away by the government. The person responsible for making the Roswell incident known to the world is the nuclear physicist Stanton Friedman.[2] He spent decades investigating Roswell and interviewing witnesses. I contacted Stan when I uncovered a fact about Roswell not known to him or to other researchers. One of my colleagues, whom I respect and who has an international reputation, told me privately that he decided to investigate the Roswell incident back in the 1970s.

This person told me that he spoke to someone who, in 1947, was a Roswell city council member. This former city council member told him that at the time of the Roswell crash, a strange event occurred that the farmers of the area were all talking about. It appears that within a short time after the crash, all the pregnant cows and sheep in the vicinity of the crash site spontaneously aborted. This had never happened there before, and it was a mystery that was discussed for some time. I also happened to talk to a woman whose father was a farmer in the Midwest during the time of the Roswell incident, and she said her father told her the same thing many years ago. I thought this would be interesting to research, as I now had two independent sources saying the same thing.

I had a great idea to track down additional information. I called the Roswell city clerk and asked him if he had a list of the city council members in 1947, and whether he could tell me who the mayor had been at that time. When he said he would get back to me, I thought I would never hear from him again, but the next day I received the list.

He said he had to go back to old microfilm copies of the city council meetings to find the names. I gave his list to a UFO researcher in
Roswell, and he is trying to track down the descendants of these people
to find out if they can corroborate the pregnant-livestock story. Who
knows what other information these individuals might reveal if they
do, in fact, come forward? Maybe they even found and kept a piece of
the Roswell crash debris, something no one claims to have today. (It's
possible that the government didn't get every piece.)

A colleague and good friend who lives in Roswell told me that some
witnesses who saw the debris claimed that there was strange writing on
some of it. At the time of the crash, in July 1947, Colonel Jesse Marcel
was the chief intelligence officer at the Roswell Army Air Field.[3] He
was the first to investigate the crash site and the crash debris found by
a man named Mac Brazel on his ranch seventy-five miles northwest of
Roswell. At first, Colonel Marcel upheld the story of the crash being
the debris of a radar reflector from a weather balloon, but thirty years
later, Colonel Marcel came forward and said the material at the Brazel
ranch had highly unusual physical properties and was definitely not a
weather balloon.

His son, Colonel Jesse Marcel Jr., who currently lives in Roswell
and is a medical doctor (ear, nose, and throat specialist and a pilot who
has served in Iraq), has recently said that his father definitely told him
that this debris was *not* of this earth. It's interesting that before Colonel
Marcel brought the debris back to the Army base, he stopped at his
house, which was on the way to the base, and brought a box of the
debris into the house to show Jesse Jr. He dumped it on the kitchen
floor and they looked through it together. His son, who was eleven at
the time, remembers this well. They both looked at it and concluded it
was not something conventional. It was not of this earth!

In 1981, about five years before Colonel Marcel died, Linda Corley
attempted to interview him. Linda was a sophomore in college at that
time, and one of her college professors told her, as an assignment, to
interview an interesting person. Jesse Marcel at that time lived in her

area in Louisiana and agreed to be interviewed. It was a four-hour, taped interview, and Linda still has those reel-to-reel tapes. Several days after the interview, Colonel Marcel called her and told her not to use it for the school project or anything else. He seemed really upset, which also upset Linda, so she put away the tapes. About seventeen years later, after the military man had passed away, she pulled them out and transcribed some of them.[4]

What is so valuable is that during the interview, Linda asked Jesse to draw the symbols on the I-beam from the alien craft as he remembered them from 1947. He actually even signed this drawing. Unfortunately, there are only six symbols in the drawing, but at least it's something. I contacted Linda through a mutual friend, and she sent me copies of some of the transcribed interview and the diagram. I found it interesting and put it away in my file. I thought it might have some relationship to Egyptian scripts but could find nothing even remotely resembling them.

In mid-July 2007, I called Stan Friedman. We had recently done a radio show together about my Roswell findings. This was a few days after he came back from the Roswell sixtieth anniversary. I asked him to send me a copy of his new book *Captured! The Betty and Barney Hill UFO Experience.*[5] This book is the story of the 1961 abduction of Betty and Barney Hill, who claimed to have been taken aboard a UFO. Later, they were not able to account for two hours of their time, and couldn't remember anything about what had happened.

About two years later, each of them separately underwent hypnosis and told the same story. They independently recalled that they had been taken aboard a UFO, where aliens probed and examined them. Betty was pregnant at the time, and she said that the aliens inserted a

Fig. 16.1. The symbols on the I-beam as recalled by Colonel Jesse Marcel Sr., and redrawn by John DeSalvo.

long needle into her abdomen. (This sounds like amniocentesis, which was not used in medicine until many years after their abduction.) The aliens also showed her a star map of their solar system, which she recalled under hypnosis. An almost exact match for this solar system was found in the Zeta Reticulum constellation system; no other known constellation came close. On board the UFO, Betty was also shown a plasticlike book, which had symbols arranged in long, narrow columns. Later, Betty re-created these symbols under hypnosis.

I had no knowledge of any of this until I read about it in Stan's new book.

I checked out the appendix of the book and was shocked to see a diagram of the symbols that Betty Hill had drawn while under hypnosis. My first impression was that they looked similar to the Marcel drawings of the symbols on the I-beam at Roswell. When I compared them side by side, I could clearly see that they were very similar indeed, and I believe they may be part of the same language. I wanted to make sure I was not fooling myself, so I asked a few other colleagues, most of whom said they also thought they were similar. They were surprised learn the source of these symbols. Even many well-known ufologists did not know of the Marcel drawings or of the Betty Hill drawings.

I called Linda Corley and asked her to check this out, since she has been studying the script and comparing it to different languages for many years. She has even published a book on it.[6] After our phone conversation, she e-mailed me to tell me that my findings were very impressive, and there were many similarities between the two drawings. Dennis Balthaser, a well-known UFO researcher, looked at it and said he definitely saw similarities between the two drawings, and that the entire matter is worthy of further study.

I was scheduled to do a radio interview that night with Stanton Friedman. I was going to talk about an unrelated topic but changed it because I was excited about my find and wanted others to know about it and get their feedback. I called Jesse Marcel Jr. before the show and asked him to look at the diagrams to see what he thought. He confirmed

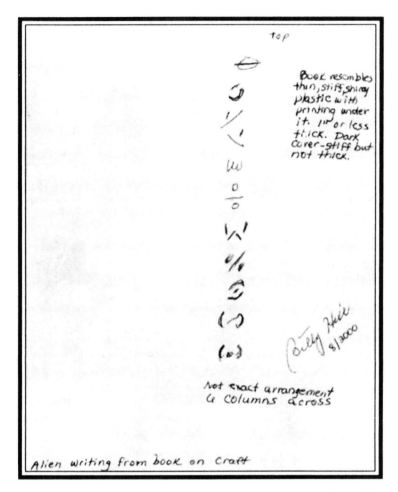

Fig. 16.2. Symbols on a book shown to Betty Hill while aboard the UFO. Image from *Captured! The Betty and Barney Hill UFO Experience*, by Stanton Friedman and Kathleen Marden. Copyright Stanton Friedman; used with permission.

the signature as his father's and believed that the drawings were consistent with his style and what he had seen in the past.

I asked him to come on the program with Stan and me, and he accepted. Three nights before, both he and Stan had been on the Larry King show together, so I felt very excited to go on national radio with these men to discuss my find.

Before I went on the air that night, however, I made another discovery. There was something familiar about Jesse Marcel's symbols—I thought they resembled something I had seen in my collection of inner writings of the Seeress. In comparing them with some of the Seeress's script, I found a few similarities in some of the numerical symbols. While there isn't an exact match, one can definitely see the similarities among the Marcel drawing, the Betty Hill drawing, and the numeric script of the Seeress.

What does this mean? My theory is that if you believe the universe is managed by angels, and they have contacted intelligent beings on Earth, wouldn't other planets have received this Primal Language? I would assume there is only one angelic language. So could this language be the link to all intelligent life in the universe? It's an interesting question to ponder. If this script on the I-beam represents some alien number, could it be a part number* or something like that? Perhaps future research will confirm these similarities and add to the evidence that we are not alone. In addition to being visited by angels, perhaps we have been visited by other intelligent life from other planets.

A REQUEST FOR HELP

Can you help decipher this language? One of the reasons I wanted to reprint every known diagram and example of the inner language of the Seeress is that someone out there, like you, may help decipher this code. If you have any interesting ideas or new discoveries, I would love to hear from you.

---

*In manufacturing, each part of an item under construction has an identifying part number. In a car, for example, each component has a number that enables the ordering of that specific part from the manufacturer.

17
THE QUEST

What are you really searching for in life? What is your true goal? Do you even know what it is? What do most people really want? Many choose money, power, sex, fame, and other materialistic things as their true goals, but are these what they really want? Do these things cover up or take the place of the true object they are searching for?

The true goal, I believe, is cosmic consciousness. It has been called by many names throughout history, including oneness with God, nirvana, satori, mystical union, enlightenment, bliss, or being one with your Holy Guardian Angel. I believe this state is not new but rather is the first and original state of humankind.

The story in Genesis of Adam and Eve in the Garden of Eden is a symbolic way of explaining it. When God first created humankind, human beings were one with God, in a state of cosmic consciousness, and communicated freely with God. They also had free will, and when they willingly left the presence of God, this state was lost. The entire quest of humankind is to regain this communion and oneness with God. That is the real goal, but we have lost sight of it and have substituted superficial and meaningless goals. The search for the original Garden of Eden represents our true search for cosmic consciousness. That's why it's important to look within ourselves to see what we truly want. What is our quest? Socrates said, "Know thyself." Perhaps this should be our first step in so doing.

Here's something to consider. Why are you reading this book? Maybe you buy other books like it, or maybe this is your first book of this kind. Do you watch unsolved mysteries on TV, or movies with metaphysical and mystical themes—for example, programs on spiritualism, magic, angels, meditations, hauntings, or ancient monuments? If so, I believe more than just mere curiosity or the desire to be entertained is driving this. You do it because you're searching for something deep within yourself, and these themes awaken that longing. They hint to you that there is a true meaning of life that you are missing.

Sometimes we are awakened to this inner longing when we lose a loved one or attend a funeral. Our thoughts turn to the spiritual questions of life, death, and the meaning of existence. Unfortunately, this feeling is not long-lived, and in a few days we are back to the hustle and bustle of the so-called real world. Maybe it's time to listen again to this voice within us and seek that which is true, infinite, and lasting.

There are many tools that can help us move toward this goal of cosmic consciousness. They're like signs pointing to the goal. One danger is that these signs are just that, *signs*. They aren't the goal, and should be used only as signs pointing out the way. We shouldn't stop and worship them, but instead move on to the next one until we reach our goal. An example of a sign pointing toward a goal is organized religion, which may be used to point us toward God. Unfortunately, some religions have become nothing more than meaningless ritual with no inner spiritual substance. They are like empty shells, and perhaps this is why most religions are quickly losing parishioners, and church and synagogue attendance is low.

Many who attend church, especially older people, may do so out of habit or because they feel guilty if they don't. Young people find that the religions that they have grown up with are meaningless and empty, and they leave to search for true meaning elsewhere. Maybe they join another religion or even a cult, where they may end up with the same problem because what they have switched to is just as meaningless and empty: it doesn't satisfy the inner longing for spiritual enlightenment.

I believe that most religions began with the purpose of helping people find union with God. They were not empty shells; the rituals were full of meaning, power, and spiritual experiences. I believe the mystics like the Seeress of Prevorst, Andrew Jackson Davis, Emanuel Swedenborg, and others have tried to rekindle the true meaning of the spiritual quest within us. They have awakened this longing in our hearts because they themselves experienced this union. It's a magical thing that can't be described in words. When you meet a happy person, you also become happy. It's contagious. When you talk to someone depressed, you tend to become depressed.

We may not have the good fortune of meeting a mystic in the flesh, but we can read about them, and many times we can read what they themselves have written. This has the same effect of awakening our spirit to higher worlds and realities and opens the true meaning of life to us. That is why we are attracted to true mystics—reading about them causes our spirit to resonate with spiritual thoughts and feelings.

When I was a college administrator, I used to take out to lunch many people with whom I did business. This included bank personnel from whom our students received loans, and other visiting college administrators and marketing people. I came into contact with all kinds of people with diverse interests and backgrounds. After small talk about the weather, sports, and hobbies was over, I would always try to move into a spiritual topic, which would depend on what I thought they might be interested in based on our conversations to date. It was like flypaper: People were attracted and drawn to a spiritual topic. They were starving for this. Typically the lunch would turn into hours instead of minutes, and they would leave with a list of books I had recommended. That is about all one could do in such a short time.

Once on an airplane, I taught someone to meditate. The person sitting next to me was a business traveler and looked stressed out. I asked him what he was doing in the next hour (ours was a three-hour flight). In that hour I taught him how to meditate, and he looked completely changed after the experience. Who knows if he continued with it and whether or not that was the beginning of his spiritual search.

We cannot predict the future. All we can do is plant the seeds and help others in their search for the truth. By helping others, we actually benefit more than they do. I believe that is a basic spiritual law. Since God is love, the more love we give, the more it is returned to us.

So, how to begin our quest? Many people begin by reading books on spirituality, metaphysics, religion, mysticism, and other similar topics. This will open up their minds and imaginations and start to make them aware of this higher spiritual world, but this is not enough. We do not advance very far on the spiritual path by just reading, although it is a good first step.

We need to turn thought into action. Many techniques are useful for opening up our communion with God. I believe meditation is extremely important, as the Seeress also said. It allows us to quiet the mind and hear that still, small voice within. Yoga is another way, and so is prayer—not the prayer of asking for things, but the prayer of quietude, or contemplation, as the mystics would describe it. Some people get involved in different aspects of the New Age. This is fine as long as one uses spiritual discernment and realizes that these are only pointers to the true goal.

The Sufis have a great saying: There are as many paths to God as souls in the world. I believe this quest is individual and can take many different routes and methods. What is right for you may not be right for someone else. What is right for you now may not be right for you a year from now. This is because we are on different spiritual levels at different times in our lives, and we continue to grow and change. A technique that may have been helpful to you at a certain time in your life will not be helpful now, since you have outgrown it and have advanced beyond it.

Even though the quest is individual, I believe there are basic aspects in common. For example, we all need exercise, but some choose running, some swimming, some tennis. As humans, we all need to eat, but we crave and need different foods. Eating is universal, but the choice of food is ours. I believe this applies to the spiritual world also. Certain things such as meditation and prayer are general practices that all can use, but the techniques are different depending on our physical, mental, and spiritual makeup.

The quest is not an intellectual pursuit. It is a real path of thoughts, words, deeds, and higher experiences. It is a transformation of the body, mind, and soul. You are being born again into a new awareness of spiritual life. Things will not be the same. You can never go home again, as the saying goes. Everything has new meaning and seems to be as it should.

How do we know we are on the right path? Again, this is personal, but I believe there are many common denominators. One is that we have feelings of peace, love, tranquillity, and the presence of God in our life. God is love, and our closeness to God will be seen by our growth in love for not only ourselves, but our fellow human beings as well. The saints exemplify this. They gave their lives for others and suffered for others. This was not something they forced themselves to do; it was natural for them—they had no other choice.

This brings us to the question that if all of us are eventually meant to have divine union with God, why should we make any effort at all? We will get there in due time. There is truth in this, but I would pose the question: Do you want to reach this goal quickly and with as little effort as possible or do you want to reach this goal in a lengthy and difficult process? I guess it's like going from point A to point B. We can run and try to do it as fast as possible using the best routes or we can use different routes that take us through many obstacles. I would like to realize this goal as quickly and as easily as possible, and I believe the spiritual path helps me to do this.

Perhaps the real question we should be asking ourselves is not about what we want, but about what do we need. All our lives we ask ourselves What do I want. But the spiritual search is different. I remember a *Twilight Zone* episode back in the 1960s about a person who knew the immediate future. He was a peddler and had a cart full of odds and ends he sold. When someone came up to him and asked him if he had this or that, he would say, You do not need that, but you need this, and he would give that person something other than what they had asked for. For example, he gave someone a pair of scissors. A few minutes later, this person went into an elevator and his tie got stuck in the door. As the elevator started to move, he was being strangled. He remembered the scissors and cut the tie and was saved. The story continued like this. So we should ask ourselves *what do I need* on my spiritual search, not what do I want.

We are not alone on this path; we will get help from others as we make an effort and progress. There is an ancient saying in the East that when the student is ready, the master will appear. This is true—we often seem to get help out of nowhere when we are in need of it. Also, God and the angels are here to help. There is a saying that for every step we take toward God, God takes ten steps toward us. I truly believe this.

The writing of this book has allowed me to take another step toward God. I hope the reading of it does the same for you and that this book has helped you on your path to divine union and cosmic consciousness.

I leave you with my favorite spiritual quotation:

I do not promise to believe tomorrow exactly what I believe today, and I do not believe today exactly what I believed yesterday. I expect to make, as I have made, some honest progress within every succeeding twenty-four hours.

—ANDREW JACKSON DAVIS, 1885

Appendix A

A MODERN PHOTO TOUR OF PREVORST AND RELATED AREAS

All photographs in appendix A are courtesy of George Setian and copyrighted by him.

Fig. A.1. A view of Prevorst.

Fig. A.2. The house where the Seeress was born is to the right of the church.

Fig. A.3. The birthplace of the Seeress, built in 1428.

Fig. A.4. Lowenstein, where the Seeress is buried, is approximately four miles from Prevorst.

Fig. A.5. The entrance to the cemetery where the Seeress is buried.

Fig. A.6. The grave and monument of the Seeress. Her body was cremated and the ashes were buried here.

Fig. A.7. A closer view of the grave of the Seeress.

Fig. A.8. Writing in gold letters on the front of the grave translates as:

Here lie the ashes
of the Seeress of Prevorst
Friedricke Hauffe born as Wanner
 Born in the year 1801.
 Died in the year 1829.

Fig. A.9. The writing on the right side of the grave translates as:

Faith and love
help even the confused [lost] soul
From a friend who thanks you
his happiness on earth
     G.V.M.

Fig. A.10. The writing on the left side of the grave translates as:

You have undone the wisdom
 of the wise;
and for your commemoration this stone
 is placed by
     G.V.M. and E.

Fig. A.11. The back of the Seeress's grave. The text is from the Seeress herself.

How am I supposed to call you
you, who aggrieve me?
I call you friends too
you have only trained [challenged] me
    Words of the Seeress.

(In German, this is a rhyme.)

Fig. A.12. The view from behind the grave.

Fig. A.13. Weinsberg: The Kerner home. Today it houses a Kerner museum. The tower on the right was added by Kerner's son twenty-two years after his father's death.

Fig. A.14. Kerner's office on the upper floor of the Kerner house. Everything is original except for the wallpaper, which is a replica of the original. It is said that the chest of drawers in the far left corner of the room is older than the house itself and quite valuable. Allegedly Kerner kept his supplies (remedies, prescriptions, chemicals for experiments, herbs, and spices) in this chest.

Fig. A.15. A portrait of Kerner from the Kerner house.

Fig. A.16. A section in the Kerner house dedicated to the Seeress. The books are Kerner's and include volumes on such topics as magnetism, ghosts, and the spiritual realm.

Fig. A.17. On one wall of the other half of the room hang diagrams that the Seeress drew. In the far corner by the window is a drawing of Friedrich Anton Mesmer. The barrel-shaped object below the drawing of Mesmer is a device that was used in the process of mesmerism. When in use, the barrel was filled with sand, and jars of glass containing river water sat atop the barrel's rim. (It is important that living water from a river be used, and not ordinary water without energy.) A rope from inside the barrel was attached to each jar. People would sit around this barrel, each of them holding a rope. The goal was for the energy of the water to be transferred through each rope to the patients.

Fig. A.18. This treatment device (discussed in chapter 3) was built by Kerner specifically for the Seeress per her instructions. Its name is *der Nervenstimmer,* which translates as "the nerve adjuster." It worked in the following manner: The glass jars contained leather from a deer, a coffin nail, and river water. (As in the case of Mesmer's device, this had to be living water from a river. The jars in the barrel of Mesmer's device are similar in shape but larger.) The glass container above the jars contained various herbs. All around its surface were holes through which the chains hung. Some of the chains on this device hung into the three jars below. All these chains and the way they were attached to the device were supposed to transfer the energy of the ingredients to the top of the triangle. At the top of the triangle there was a cord. This cord was meant to transfer the energy onto the patient. Before this could happen, however, the ingredients had to be "activated" by a magnet, which you can see. Kerner would hold the heavy magnet to the jars and their ingredients, and would run it all over the device. After that, the device could be used. Thus, this device worked by tapping in to the magnetic energy of certain ingredients and using their power for healing.

Fig. A.19. In the corner where the table is and beside the closed window is where stood the bed of the Seeress.

Appendix B

Fr⊕m the Seeress's J⊕urnal

The following text contains dated excerpts from the Seeress's journal, preceded and followed by explanatory paragraphs from Dr. Kerner.[1]

Mrs. H. [Kerner referred to the Seeress in his writings as Mrs. H., for Hauffe] kept a journal for some weeks whilst she was in Weinsberg, which she reserved entirely for herself and allowed nobody to see. As she grew weaker, she was unable to continue it; and I got possession of the papers unknown to her. In order to exhibit the state of her mind, and to prove that the desire to return to her home and husband was her ruling feeling, a point on which she has been much misunderstood, as well as to show her entire conviction of the reality of the apparitions, I will extract the following passage, which she never intended should meet any eye but her own. [Dr. Justinus Kerner]

December 26, 1827—Speechless paper! To thee I fly for refuge! How gladly I would impart my experiences and the feelings of my soul, to a friend to whom I could open my heart, and disclose my innermost thoughts—one whose soul was in harmony with mine, and who could afford me comfort and consolation under my sufferings! Is it my fault that I have no such friend? Is it that I am too timid, or that I place too little confidence in the friends I have? I do not think this is natural to me; but I am repelled by finding that I am so seldom understood, and so often misinterpreted. But it is my joy to feel that there is *one* who sees me, and knows me; his I am, and will remain— thine, Father in heaven!

December 27, 1827—Today my conviction is again confirmed that we live in a transitory, imperfect world; and that we can rely on nothing that *lives* and *weaves* in it; but must put our trust only in that which we do not see—namely, the Word, the truth, and eternal life. By holding fast to this, one is enabled to support the abandonment in which I find myself, and the separation from all I love; and the soul is ever more and more drawn to the spirit. The body indeed becomes weaker—especially mine, which is already so weak. Such a friend were indeed a comfort!—one whom I could call the friend of my soul, and to whom I could communicate all my feelings.

Today I had a visit from a very disquieting apparition, which concerns K., for it is that of a relation of his. This spirit, who was a mother (I knew her when alive), wishes me, through K. to warn her children that there is a future life, and that if they do not turn to their Redeemer, they will taste, even more than she does, the bitterness of death. So says this spirit. What shall I do? God assist me to do right!

December 28, 1827—Last night the spectre [spirit] came again to remind me what I should do.

December 29, 1827—Today I seemed very cheerful, but towards evening I was seized with a fearful homesickness. If this continue, my health will become worse. I must seek comfort in myself, for nobody can help me. When people speak to me as they do in the world, I only grow sadder. Would I could always cling to my Redeemer, but I am timid and sinful.

The spirit came again at eleven o'clock today, and said, with a threatening aspect, "Will you not do what I desire?" I answered, "I cannot; go to K. yourself." As I said this, it disappeared. I am perplexed what to do, people will not believe. In the name of God they may, for I am convinced it is true; but this spirit-seeing costs me much pain. (Mrs. H. here alluded to my frequent reproaches, and arguments against the validity of the spectres.)

January 1, 1828—I passed this day alone with my old waiting woman, mostly in reflection; and the following ideas occurred to me: "Man, set thy house in order, for thou must die." Whereon it struck me, that we should do this daily, keeping the image of death ever before us. At half-past eleven, that spirit came, and said, "How long will you withhold me from my rest?" I appeased it by saying, I would obey it; but when, heaven knows. I hope it will come no more.

January 2, 1828—Last night, the spirit returned with its usual request. I promised to do its bidding the next day; and it left me cheerfully. But in the morning, my heart failed me; I was sad, and wished myself home. He, who alone knows me, and my sufferings, grant this!

January 5, 1828—I have not slept from bodily weakness and affliction. I wept nearly all night. How should I recover my health? At one o'clock came that bright form that has often appeared to me before, like a consoling angel; it said, "Be calm; by to-morrow evening things will be better with you. Help approaches." It said other things too which I treasure in my heart.

January 6, 1828—I have been better today, with the exception of my homesickness. Just when that was at the worst, in came my husband, and my heart grew light at once. I thought of the assurance of the bright form, that the evening would bring me comfort.

January 7, 1828—This has been a tolerably comfortable day, God be thanked! For my husband remained with me, and shared the burden of my pains and afflictions.

January 8, 1828—I have not slept all night for spasms, thinking of my husband's approaching departure. At mid-day he left me, and I am again alone. Father in heaven! witness my tears, and give me strength to support my troubles. Grant me patience to bear the burden thou hast laid upon me, for thou alone knowest me! Mankind will not understand me.

With regard to the request of the spectre above mentioned, which occasioned Mrs. H. so much anxiety, it is a remarkable fact, that shortly afterwards a circumstance occurred to one of the children of this spirit, which evinced his want of trust in God; whilst, at the same time, there was so incomprehensible an instance of the preservation of life, that it could hardly fail to produce belief in the existence of a superintending Providence. [Dr. Kerner]

Appendix C

POETRY OF THE
SEERESS

The following is a sample of poetry written by the Seeress, composed immediately before her death. It was translated by Catherine Crowe.[1]

> *Oh! Father, thou only knowest my heart,*
> *And whether I deceive—*
> *Whether the secrets I impart*
> *Are truths, or lies I weave.*

> *Alas! although from thee I hold*
> *The dreadful power to unfold*
> *The secrets of the grave;*
> *Gladly would I that gift resign,*
> *And close this inner-eye of mine—*
> *But not my will be done, but thine.*

> *Farewell! dear friends! farewell!*
> *Thanks for your love and tending*
> *Of the weary life now ending—*
> *Farewell! farewell!*

And shall I call ye friends,
Sent for the wisest ends,
To aggravate my woes?
Yes, friends no less than those—
Farewell! farewell!

Farewell to all I love!
Whilst my spirit floats above.
My body'll here remain
To witness my life of pain*—
Farewell! farewell!

Grieve not that I'm at rest!
Farewell all I love best!
Soon we shall meet again
Where dwells no grief nor pain—
Farewell! farewell!

---

*The Seeress here refers to a wish she had expressed that her body should be opened.

N⊕TES

PREFACE

1. DeSalvo, *Andrew Jackson Davis: First American Prophet and Clairvoyant.*

CHAPTER 1. THE LANGUAGE OF THE SPIRITS

1. Genesis 2:19 (King James Version).
2. Ibid., 5:4 (KJV).
3. Ibid., 5:24 (KJV).
4. Ibid., 7:9 (KJV).
5. Ibid., 11:1 (KJV).
6. Matthew 8:8 (KJV).
7. Personal communications, 2007.

CHAPTER 2. INTRODUCTION TO THE SEERESS

1. Kerner, *The Seeress of Prevorst: Being Revelations Concerning the Inner-Life of Man, and the Inter-Diffusion of a World of Spirits in the One We Inhabit.*
2. Howitt, *The History of the Supernatural.*
3. Ibid., 63.

4. Kerner, *Die Seherin von Prevorst: Eröffnungen über das innere Leben des Menschen und über das Hereinragen einer Geisterwelt in die unsere.*
5. Ibid., *The Seeress of Prevorst*, 191.
6. Ibid., *The Seeress of Prevorst.*
7. Fuller, *Summer on the Lakes*, 125.
8. Ibid., 165.

CHAPTER 3. THE LIFE OF THE SEERESS

1. Kerner, *The Seeress of Prevorst.*
2. Ibid., 33.
3. Ibid.
4. Ibid., 34–35.
5. Ibid., 36–37.
6. Ibid., 43–44.
7. Ibid., 44.
8. Ibid., 45.
9. Ibid., 46–47.
10. Ibid., 49.
11. Ibid., 50–51.
12. Ibid., 51–52.
13. Ibid., 53, 54.
14. Ibid., 56.

CHAPTER 4. MESMERISM AND HYPNOSIS

1. Barter, *How to Hypnotise Including the Whole Art of Mesmerism.*
2. Sugrue, *There Is a River: The Story of Edgar Cayce.*
3. DeSalvo, *Andrew Jackson Davis.*
4. Kirkpatrick, *Edgar Cayce: An American Prophet,* 143.
5. Coates, *How to Mesmerise.*
6. Barter, *How to Hypnotise Including the Whole Art of Mesmerism.*
7. Carpenter, *Plain Instructions in Hypnotism and Mesmerism* (Boston: Lee and Shepard, 1900).
8. Barter, *How to Hypnotise Including the Whole Art of Mesmerism.*
9. H. P. Blavatsky, "Psychic and Noetic Action," in *Lucifer.*

CHAPTER 5. CLAIRVOYANCE

1. Kerner, *The Seeress of Prevorst.*
2. Ibid., 24.
3. Genesis 28:12 (KJV).
4. Kerner, *The Seeress of Prevorst,* 25–26.
5. Bucke, *Cosmic Consciousness: A Study in the Evolution of the Human Mind.*
6. Kerner, *The Seeress of Prevorst,* 26.
7. Ibid., 27.
8. Ibid., 29.
9. DeSalvo, *Decoding the Pyramids,* 144–45.
10. Kerner, *The Seeress of Prevorst,* 29.
11. Devereux, *Places of Power: Measuring the Secret Energy of Ancient Sites.*

12. Kirkpatrick, *Edgar Cayce: An American Prophet,* 130.
13. Kerner, *The Seeress of Prevorst,* 23–24.
14. Ibid., 56–57.
15. Ibid., 57.
16. Ibid., 59.
17. Ibid., 60.

CHAPTER 6. SPIRIT SEEING

1. Kerner, *The Seeress of Prevorst.*
2. Ibid., 60.
3. Ibid., 156–61.
4. Ibid., 163–64.
5. Ibid., 3.
6. Ibid.
7. Mahan, *Modern Mysteries Explained and Exposed.*
8. Kerner, *The Seeress of Prevorst,* 3–4.
9. Ibid., 4.
10. Ibid., 110.

CHAPTER 7. SPIRITUALISM

1. I Samuel, chapter 28 (KJV).
2. DeSalvo, *Andrew Jackson Davis,* ch. 7.
3. Kase, *The Emancipation Proclamation.*
4. Maynard, *Was Abraham Lincoln a Spiritualist?,* 71–73.
5. Ibid.
6. DeSalvo, *Andrew Jackson Davis,* 100.
7. Leale, personal communications, 2004.
8. Emerson, personal communications, 2005, 2006.

CHAPTER 8. DEVELOPMENT OF THE INNER LIFE

1. Kerner, *The Seeress of Prevorst,* 5.
2. Teresa of Avila, *The Life of Saint Teresa of Avila by Herself.*
3. Kerner, *The Seeress of Prevorst,* 5.
4. Ibid., 6.
5. Ibid.
6. Ibid.
7. Ibid., 6–7.
8. Ibid., 9–10.
9. Matthew 11:15 (KJV).
10. Kerner, *The Seeress of Prevorst*, 14.
11. Ibid., 15.
12. Ibid., 19.
13. Ibid., 21.

CHAPTER 9. SPIRITUAL SENSITIVITIES

1. Exodus 28:30 (KJV).
2. Kerner, *The Seeress of Prevorst,* 62.
3. Ibid., 63–65.
4. DeSalvo, *Andrew Jackson Davis*, ch. 6.
5. Kerner, *The Seeress of Prevorst,* 74–75.
6. Ibid., 77.
7. Ibid., 80.
8. Ibid., 81.
9. Ibid., 86–88.
10. Ibid., 92.
11. Ibid., 93.
12. Ibid., 94.
13. Ibid., 95.
14. Ibid., 96.
15. Ibid.
16. Ibid., 98.

CHAPTER 10. INNER LANGUAGE AND NUMBERS

1. Kerner, *The Seeress of Prevorst.*
2. Ibid., 127.
3. Ibid., 128.
4. Ibid., 118.

CHAPTER 11. THE SUN AND LIFE SPHERES

1. Kerner, *The Seeress of Prevorst.*
2. Ibid., 128.
3. Ibid., 120.
4. Ibid., 121.
5. DeSalvo, *Andrew Jackson Davis.*
6. Kerner, *The Seeress of Prevorst,* 122.
7. Ibid., 139.
8. Ibid.
9. Ibid., 122.
10. Howitt, *The History of the Supernatural in All Ages and Nations,* 92.
11. Kerner, *The Seeress of Prevorst,* 140.
12. Ibid., 141.

CHAPTER 12. MAGIC AND MAGICAL SCRIPTS

1. Regardie, *The Tree of Life: An Illustrated Study in Magic.*
2. C. F. Smith, *John Dee.*
3. Ibid., 8.
4. Ibid.
5. Deacon, *John Dee: Scientist, Geographer, Astrologer and Secret Agent to Elizabeth I.*
6. Dee, *The Mathematical Praeface to*

the Elements of Geometrie of Euclid
of Megara (1570).

7. Dee, *A True and Faithful Relation
of What Passed for Many Years
Between Dr. John Dee and Some
Spirits.*

CHAPTER 13. THE VOYNICH
MANUSCRIPT

1. Kennedy and Churchill, *The
Voynich Manuscript.*

2. www.voynich.nu.

3. Personal communication of the
author, 2007.

4. www.voynich.nu.

CHAPTER 14. THE DEATH
OF THE SEERESS

1. Kerner, *The Seeress of Prevorst,*
144.

2. Ibid., 145.

3. Ibid., 331.

4. Ibid., 146.

5. Ibid., 149.

CHAPTER 15. DR. KERNER AND
HIS INNER CIRCLE

1. Watts, *The Pioneers of the
Spiritual Reformation: Life and
Works of Dr. Justinus Kerner and
William Howitt and His Work for
Spiritualism.*

2. Kerner, *Die Seherin von Prevorst.*

3. Kerner, *The Seeress of Prevorst.*

4. Howitt, *The History of the
Supernatural,* vol. 1, 62.

5. Watts, *The Pioneers of the Spiritual
Reformation.*

6. Ibid., 12.

7. Ibid., 16.

8. Ibid., 23.

9. Ibid., 32.

CHAPTER 16. FINAL THOUGHTS
AND SPECULATIONS

1. Abbott, *Flatland: A Romance of
Many Dimensions.*

2. Friedman, *Crash at Corona:
The U.S. Military Retrieval and
Cover-Up of a UFO.*

3. Marcel, *The Roswell Legacy.*

4. Corley, *For the Sake of My Country:
An Intimate Conversation with
Lieutenant Colonel Jesse A. Marcel,
Senior.*

5. Friedman and Marden, *Captured!
The Betty and Barney Hill UFO
Experience.*

6. Corley, *For the Sake of My Country.*

APPENDIX B: FROM THE
SEERESS'S JOURNAL

1. Kerner, *The Seeress of Prevorst,*
321–25.

APPENDIX C: POETRY
OF THE SEERESS

1. Kerner, *The Seeress of Prevorst,* 337,
338.

BIBLI⊕GRAPHY

Abbott, Edwin A. *Flatland: A Romance of Many Dimensions.* New York: Barnes and Noble, 1963.

Barter, John. *How to Hypnotise Including the Whole Art of Mesmerism.* London: Simpkin, Marshall, Hamilton, Kent & Co., 1890.

Blavatsky, H. P. "Psychic and Noetic Action." *Lucifer* (October–November 1890).

Bucke, Richard Maurice. *Cosmic Consciousness: A Study in the Evolution of the Human Mind.* Philadelphia: Innes and Sons, 1901.

Carpenter, A. E. *Plain Instructions in Hypnotism and Mesmerism.* Boston: Lee and Shepard, 1900.

Coates, James. *How to Mesmerise.* London: W. Foulsham and Co., 1899.

Corley, Linda G. *For the Sake of My Country: An Intimate Conversation with Lieutenant Colonel Jesse A. Marcel, Senior.* Bloomington, Ind.: AuthorHouse, 2007.

Davis, Andrew Jackson. *The Principles of Nature, Her Divine Revelations and a Voice to Mankind.* London: John Chapman, 1847.

Deacon, Richard. *John Dee: Scientist, Geographer, Astrologer and Secret Agent to Elizabeth I.* London: Frederick Muller, 1968.

Dee, John. *The Mathematical Praeface to the Elements of Geometrie of Euclid of Megara (1570),* with an introduction by Allen G. Debus. New York: Science Historical Publications, 1975.

———. *A True and Faithful Relation of What Passed for Many Years Between Dr. John Dee and Some Spirits.* London: D. Maxwell, 1659.

DeSalvo, John. *Andrew Jackson Davis: First American Prophet and Clairvoyant.* Morrisville, N.C.: Lulu, 2005.

———. *Decoding the Pyramids.* New York: Barnes and Noble, 2008.

Devereux, Paul. *Places of Power: Measuring the Secret Energy of Ancient Sites.* London: Blanford, 1999.

Friedman, Stanton. *Crash at Corona: The U.S. Military Retrieval and Cover-Up of a UFO.* New York: Paraview Special Editions, 2004.

Friedman, Stanton T., and Kathleen Marden. *Captured! The Betty and Barney Hill UFO Experience.* Franklin Lakes, N.J.: New Page Books, 2007.

Fuller, Margaret. *Summer on the Lakes.* New York: Charles C. Little and James Brown, 1843.

Howitt, William. *The History of the Supernatural in All Ages and Nations.* London: Longman, Green, Longman, Roberts & Green, 1863.

Kase, Colonel Simon P. *The Emancipation Proclamation.* Philadelphia: Colonel S. P. Kase, 1898.

Kennedy, Gerry, and Rob Churchill. *The Voynich Manuscript: The Mysterious Code That Has Defied Interpretation for Centuries.* Rochester, Vt.: Inner Traditions, 2006.

Kerner, Justinus. *The Seeress of Prevorst: Being Revelations Concerning the Inner-Life of Man, and the Inter-Diffusion of a World of Spirits in the One We Inhabit.* Translated by Catherine Crowe. London: J. C. Moore, 1845, 1855, 1859.

———. *Die Seherin von Prevorst: Eröffnungen über das innere Leben des Menschen und über das Hereinragen einer Geisterwelt in die unsere.* Stuttgart, Germany: Cotta, 1829, 1832, 1838, 1846.

———. *Die Seherin von Prevorst.* Leipzig, Germany: n.p., 1920.

Kirkpatrick, Sidney D. *Edgar Cayce: An American Prophet.* New York: Riverhead Books, 2000.

Korte, Anne-Marie. "A Woman Alone: The Beatification of Frederika Hauffe nee Wanner 1801–1829." In *Women and Miracle Stories: A Multidisciplinary Exploration.* Boston: Brill, 2001.

Kretschmar, F. *Die Seherin von Prevorst und die Botschaft Justinus Kerners.* Weinsberg, Germany: 1929.

Mahan, Reverend A. *Modern Mysteries Explained and Exposed.* Cleveland: John P. Jewett and Company, 1855.

Marcel, Jesse, Jr. *The Roswell Legacy.* Franklin Lakes, N.J.: Career Press, 2009.

Maynard, Nettie Colburn. *Was Abraham Lincoln a Spiritualist?* Philadelphia: Rufus C. Hartranft, 1891.

Ossoli, Margaret Fuller. *At Home and Abroad.* Boston: The Tribune Association, 1869.

Regardie, Israel. *The Tree of Life: An Illustrated Study in Magic.* London: Rider & Co., 1932.

Sargent, E., and Robert Brothers. *Planchette; or, The Despair of Science, Being a Full Account of Modern Spiritualism, Its Phenomena, and the Various Theories Regarding It.* Boston: Robert Brothers, 1869.

"The Seeress of Prevorst." *Littell's Living Age* 6 (1845): 171–74.

"The Seeress of Prevorst." *Tait's Edinburgh Magazine* 12, no. 9 (September 1845): 586–91.

Smith, Charlotte Fell. *John Dee.* London: Constable and Company, 1900.

Smith, Eleanor Touhey. "A Medical Puzzle: Frederika Hauffe; Seeress of Prevorst." In *Psychic People.* New York: Bantam Books, 1969.

Sugrue, Thomas. *There Is a River: The Story of Edgar Cayce.* New York: Holt, Rinehart and Winston, 1942.

"Supernatural Appearances: The Seeress of Prevorst." *The New Jerusalem Magazine* 21 (August 1848): 409–17.

Teresa of Avila. *The Life of Saint Teresa of Avila by Herself.* New York: Penguin Classics, 1988.

Tuttle, Hudson. *Arcana of Nature,* vol. 1. Boston: William White & Co., 1870.

Watts, Anna Mary Howitt. *The Pioneers of the Spiritual Reformation: Life and Works of Dr. Justinus Kerner and William Howitt and His Work for Spiritualism.* London: The Psychological Press Association, 1883.

Wilson, James Victor. *How to Magnetize, or Magnetism and Clairvoyance.* New York: Fowler and Wells Co., 1890.

Young, Martin. *The Secrets of Clairvoyance and How to Become an Operator.* Baltimore: I & M Ottenheimer, 1884.

About the Author

John DeSalvo is the author of *The Complete Pyramid Sourcebook,* contributing science editor for the book *SINDON: A Layman's Guide to the Shroud of Turin,* and coauthor of *Human Anatomy: A Study Guide.* His book *Andrew Jackson Davis: The First American Prophet and Clairvoyant* reveals for the first time the scientific prophecies of Andrew Jackson Davis and his revelations about death and the afterlife. His most recent work, *Decoding the Pyramids,* is a full-color illustrated book on the Great Pyramid, pyramid research, and pyramids around the world.

A former college professor and administrator, DeSalvo holds a Ph.D. degree in biophysics. He was a recipient of research grants and fellowships from the National Science Foundation (NSF), United States Public Health (USPH), and the National Institutes of Health (NIH).

For over twenty years, Dr. DeSalvo was one of the scientists involved in studying the Shroud of Turin. Currently, he is executive vice president of ASSIST (Association of Scientists and Scholars International for the Shroud of Turin), the largest and oldest research association in the United States currently studying the Shroud of Turin. DeSalvo is also director of the Great Pyramid of Giza Research Association. He makes frequent radio appearances to discuss numerous topics, among them pyramid research, the Shroud of Turin, Andrew Jackson Davis, and Abraham Lincoln.

His websites are www.gizapyramid.com and www.andrewjacksondavis.com.

INDEX